OLD MOORE'S

HOROSCOPE AND ASTRAL DIARY

CANCER

OLD MOORE'S

HOROSCOPE AND ASTRAL DIARY

CANCER

foulsham

LONDON • NEW YORK • TORONTO • SYDNEY

foulsham

The Publishing House, Bennetts Close,
Cippenham, Slough, Berks SL1 5AP, England

Foulsham books can be found in all good bookshops or direct from
www.foulsham.com

ISBN 13: 978-0-572-03242-5
ISBN 10: 0-572-03242-0

Printed in Great Britain by Cox & Wyman Ltd, Reading, Berkshire.

CONTENTS

INTRODUCTION

Astrology has been a part of life for centuries now, and no matter how technological our lives become, it seems that it never diminishes in popularity. For thousands of years people have been gazing up at the star-clad heavens and seeing their own activities and proclivities reflected in the movement of those little points of light. Across centuries countless hours have been spent studying the way our natures, activities and decisions seem to be paralleled by their predictable movements. Old Moore, a time-served veteran in astrological research, continues to monitor the zodiac and has produced the Astral Diary for 2007, tailor-made to your own astrological make-up.

Old Moore's Astral Diary is unique in its ability to get to the heart of your nature and to offer you the sort of advice that might come from a trusted friend. The Diaries are structured in such a way that you can see in a day-by-day sense exactly how the planets are working for you. The diary section advises how you can get the best from upcoming situations and allows you to plan ahead successfully. There is room in the daily sections to put your own observations or even appointments, and the book is conveniently structured to stay with you throughout the year.

Whilst other popular astrology books merely deal with your astrological 'Sun sign', the Astral Diaries go much further. Every person on the planet is unique, and Old Moore allows you to access your individuality in a number of ways. The front section gives you the chance to work out the placement of the Moon at the time of your birth and to see how its position has set an important seal on your overall nature. Perhaps most important of all, you can use the Astral Diary to discover your Rising Sign. This is the zodiac sign that was appearing over the Eastern horizon at the time of your birth and is just as important to you as an individual as is your Sun sign.

It is the synthesis of many different astrological possibilities that makes you what you are, and with the Astral Diaries you can learn so much. How do you react to love and romance? Through the unique Venus tables and the readings that follow them, you can learn where the planet Venus was at the time of your birth. It is even possible to register when little Mercury appears to be running retrograde, which can explain why you sometimes feel chatty, whilst at other moments you would rather withdraw into yourself. The Astral Diary will be an interest and a support throughout the whole year ahead.

Old Moore extends his customary greeting to all people of the Earth and offers his age-old wishes for a happy and prosperous period ahead.

THE ESSENCE
OF CANCER

Exploring the Personality of
Cancer the Crab

(22ND JUNE – 22ND JULY)

What's in a sign?

The most obvious fact about you, particularly when viewed by others, is that you are trustworthy. Sometimes this fact gets on your nerves. Many Cancerians long to be bigger, bolder and more ruthless, but it simply isn't the way you were made. You are basically ruled by your emotions and there is very little you can do to get away from the fact. Once you realise this you could be in for a happy life but there are bound to be some frustrations on the way.

Your ruling planet is the Moon, which changes its position in astrological terms far more quickly than any other heavenly body. That's why you can sometimes feel that you have experienced a whole year's emotions in only a month. However the saving grace of this fact is that unlike the other Water signs of Scorpio and Pisces, you are rarely bogged down by emotional restraints for more than a day or two at a time. This gives you a more optimistic attitude and a determination to use your natural talents to the full, even in the face of some adversity. Caring for others is second nature to you and forms a very large part of your life and character.

Your attitude towards romance fluctuates but is generally of the 'story book' sort. Once you commit yourself to another person, either romantically or practically, you are not likely to change your mind very easily. Loyalty is part of what you are about and doesn't change just because things sometimes get a little complicated. Even when you don't really know where you are going, you are inclined to pull those you love along the path with you, and you can usually rely on their assistance. Basically you are very easy to love and there can't be anything much wrong with that fact. At the same time you can be very practical, don't mind doing some of the dirty work and are in your element when those around you are floundering.

The creative potential within your nature is strong. You are a natural homemaker and tend to get a great deal from simply watching others succeed. All the same this isn't the whole story because you are complex and inclined to be too worrisome.

Cancer resources

Your ruling planet is the Moon, Earth's closest neighbour in space. This means that you are as subject to its tides and fluctuations as is our planet. Of course this is a double-edged sword because you can sometimes be an emotional maelstrom inside. To compensate for this fact you have a level of personal sensitivity that would be admired by many. At the same time you have a deep intuition and can usually be relied upon to see through the mist of everyday life and to work out how situations are likely to mature. This is especially true when it comes to assessing those around you.

As a homemaker you are second to none. You can make a few pounds go a very long way and can cope well in circumstances that would greatly trouble those around you. Adversity is not something that bothers you too much at all and it is clear that you can even revel in difficulty. Nothing is too much trouble when you are dealing with people you really love – which includes friends as well as family members.

One of the greatest Cancerian resources is the ability to bring a practical face to even difficult circumstances. Physically speaking you are very resilient, even if you don't always seem to be the strongest person around in an emotional sense. You are given to showing extreme kindness, sometimes even in the face of cruelty from others, though if you are genuinely provoked you can show an anger that would shock most people, even those who think they know you very well indeed.

What really counts the most is your ability to bring others round to your point of view and to get them to do what you think is best. Working from example you won't generally expect others to do anything you are not prepared to try yourself, and your attitude can be an inspiration to others. Through hard work and perseverance you can build a good life for yourself, though your consideration for those around you never diminishes and so even a fortune gained would generally be used on behalf of the world around you. The greatest resource that you possess is your capacity to love and to nurture. This makes you successful and well loved by others.

Beneath the surface

The most difficult aspect of those born under the sign of Cancer the Crab is trying to work out the psychological motivations of this apparently simple but actually deeply complex zodiac position. 'Emotion' is clearly the keyword and is the fountain from which everything, good and bad alike, flows. Whilst some zodiac sign types are inclined to act and then consider the consequences, the Crab is a different beast altogether. The main quality of Cancer is caring. This applies as much to the world at large as it does in consideration of family, though to the Crab it's clear that under almost all circumstances family comes first.

You are a deep thinker and don't always find it easy to explain the way your mind is working. The reason for this is not so difficult to understand. Feelings are not the same as thoughts and it is sometimes quite difficult to express the qualities that rule you internally. What you seem to prefer to do is to put a caring arm around the world and express your inner compassion in this manner. You might also sometimes be a little anxious that if others knew how your innermost mind worked you would become more vulnerable than you already are – which is why the Crab wears a shell in the first place.

At the first sign of emotional pressure from outside you are inclined to retreat into yourself. As a result you don't always confront issues that would be best dealt with immediately. This proclivity runs deep and strong in your nature and can sometimes cause you much more trouble than would be the case if you just made the right statements and asked the correct questions. Physically and mentally you are not inclined to withdraw because you are very much stronger than the world would give you credit for.

Cancerians have a tremendous capacity to love, allied to a potential for positive action when the lives or well-being of others is threatened. In some ways you are the bravest zodiac sign of all because you will march forward into the very gates of hell if you know that you can be of service to those around you. From family to village or town, from town to nation and from nation to a global awareness, yours is the zodiac sign that best epitomises humanity's struggle for a universal understanding.

Making the best of yourself

If you start out from the premise that you are well liked by most people then you are halfway towards any intended destination. Of course you don't always register your popularity and are given to worrying about the impression you give. The picture you paint of yourself is usually very different from the one the world at large sees. If you doubt this, ask some of your best friends to describe your nature and you will be quite surprised. You need to be as open as possible to avoid internalising matters that would be best brought into a more public arena. Your natural tendency to look after everyone else masks a desire to get on in life personally, and the Cancerians who succeed the best are the ones who have somehow managed to bring a sense of balance to their giving and taking.

Try to avoid being too quiet. In social situations you have much to offer, though would rarely do so in a particularly gregarious manner. Nevertheless, and partly because you don't shoot your mouth off all the time, people are willing to listen to what you have to say. Once you realise how strong your influence can be you are already on the road to riches – financial and personal.

Use your imagination to the full because it is one of the most potent weapons in your personal armoury. People won't underestimate you when they know how strong you really are and that means that life can sometimes be less of a struggle. But under most circumstances be your usual warm self, and the love you desire will come your way.

The very practical issues of life are easy for you to deal with, which is why your material success is generally assured. All that is needed to make the picture complete is more confidence in your ability to lead and less inclination to follow.

The impressions you give

There is no doubt at all that you are one of the most loved and the most admired people around. It isn't hard to see why. Your relatives and friends alike feel very protected and loved, which has got to be a good start when it comes to your contacts with the world at large.

The most intriguing thing about being a Cancerian subject is how different you appear to be when viewed by others as against the way you judge your own personality. This is down to external appearances as much as anything. For starters you usually wear a cheery smile, even on those occasions when it is clear you are not smiling inside. You give yourself fully to the needs and wants of those around you and are very sympathetic, even towards strangers. It's true that you may not fully exploit the implications of your pleasant nature – but that's only another typical part of your character.

Those people who know you the best are aware that you have a great capacity to worry about things, and they may also understand that you are rarely as confident as you give the external impression of being. They sense the deeply emotional quality of your nature and can observe the long periods of deep thought. When it comes to the practicalities of life, however, you perhaps should not be surprised that you are sometimes put on rather too much. Even this is understandable because you rarely say no and will usually make yourself available when there is work to be done.

True success for the Cancer subject lies in recognising your strong points and in being willing to gain from them in a personal sense from time to time. You also need to realise that, to others, the impression you give is what you really are. Bridging the gap between outward calm and inner confusion might be the most important lesson.

The way forward

Although you don't always feel quite as sure of yourself as you give the impression of being, you can still exploit your external appearance to your own and other people's advantage. Your strong sense of commitment to family and your ability to get on well in personal relationships are both factors that improve your ability to progress in life. Achieving a sense of balance is important. For example you can spend long hours locked into your own thoughts, but this isn't good for you in an exclusive sense. Playing out some of your fantasies in the real world can do you good, even though you are aware that this involves taking chances, something you don't always care to do. At the same time you should not be afraid to make gains as a result of the way you are loved by others. This doesn't come for free and you work long and hard to establish the affection that comes your way.

In practical matters you are capable and well able to get on in life. Money comes your way, not usually as a result of particularly good luck, but because you are a tireless and steady worker. You can accept responsibility, even though the implied management side of things worries you somewhat. To have a career is important because it broadens your outlook and keeps you functioning in the wider world, which is where your personal successes take place. The more you achieve, the greater is the level of confidence that you feel – which in turn leads to even greater progress.

Cancerians should never cut themselves off from the mainstream of life. It's true you have many acquaintances but very few really close friends, but that doesn't matter. Practically everyone you know is pleased to name you as a trusted ally, which has to be the best compliment of all to your apparently serene and settled nature.

In love you are ardent and sincere. It may take you a while to get round to expressing the way you feel, partly because you are a little afraid of failure in this most important area of your life. All the same you love with a passion and are supportive to your partner. Family will always be the most important sphere of life because your zodiac sign rules the astrological fourth house, which is essentially dedicated to home and family matters. If you are contented in this arena it tends to show in other areas of your life too. Your affable nature is your best friend and only tends to disappear if you allow yourself to become too stressed.

CANCER ON THE CUSP

Old Moore is often asked how astrological profiles are altered for those people born at either the beginning or the end of a zodiac sign, or, more properly, on the cusps of a sign. In the case of Cancer this would be on the 22nd of June and for two or three days after, and similarly at the end of the sign, probably from the 20th to the 22nd of July. In this year's Astral Diaries, once again, Old Moore sets out to explain the differences regarding cuspid signs.

The Gemini Cusp – June 22nd to June 24th

You are certainly fun to be around and the sign of Gemini has a great deal to do with your basic motivations. As a result, you tend to be slightly more chatty than the average Cancerian and usually prove to be the life and soul of any party that is going on in your vicinity. Not everyone understands the basic sensitivity that lies below the surface of this rather brash exterior, however, and you can sometimes be a little hurt if people take you absolutely at face value.

There probably isn't the total consistency of emotional responses that one generally expects to find in the Crab when taken alone, and there are times when you might be accused of being rather fickle. All the same, you have a big heart and show genuine concern for anyone in trouble, especially the underdog. Your Gemini attributes give you the opportunity to speak your mind, so when it comes to aiding the world you can be a tireless reformer and show a great ability to think before you speak, which is not typical of Gemini on its own, although there are occasions when the two sides of your nature tend to be at odds with each other.

At work you are very capable and can be relied upon to make instant decisions whenever necessary. Your executive capabilities are pronounced and you are more than capable of thinking on your feet, even if you prefer to mull things over if possible. You are the sort of person that others tend to rely on for advice and will not usually let your colleagues or friends down.

In matters of love, you are less steadfast and loyal than the Crab, yet you care very deeply for your loved ones. People like to have you around and actively seek your advice which, in the main, is considered and sound, though always delivered with humour. You love to travel and would never wish to be limited in either your horizons or your lifestyle. All in all, you are a fun person, good to know, and basically sensible.

The Leo Cusp – July 20th to July 22nd

Here we find a Cancerian who tends to know what he or she wants from life. Part of the natural tendency of the Crab is to be fairly shy and retiring, though progressively less so as the Sun moves on towards the sign of Leo. You are probably aware that you don't exactly match the Cancer stereotype and are likely to be more outspoken, determined and even argumentative at times. You have lofty ideals, which find a ready home for the sensitive qualities that you draw from Cancer. Many social reformers tend to have their Suns very close to the Leo cusp of Cancer and people born on this cusp like to work hard for the world, especially for the less well-off members of society.

In matters of love, you are deep, but ardent and sincere, finding better ways of expressing your emotions verbally than those generally associated with the Crab. You are capable at work, easily able to take on responsibilities that involve controlling other people, and you are outwardly braver than often seems to be the case with Cancer alone. Not everyone finds you particularly easy to understand, probably because there are some definite paradoxes about your nature.

A few problems come along in the area of ideals, which are more important to you than they would be to some of the people with whom you associate. You need to be sure of yourself, a fact that leads to fairly long thinking periods, but once you have formed a particular belief you will move heaven and earth to demonstrate how sensible it is. Don't be too alarmed if not everyone agrees with you.

You are not the typical conformist that might more usually be the case with Cancerians, and feel the need to exercise your civic rights to the full. Tireless when dealing with something you think is especially important, you are a good and loyal friend, a staunch and steadfast lover and you care deeply about your family. However, you are not as confrontational as a person born completely under Leo, and therefore can usually be relied upon to seek a compromise.

CANCER AND ITS ASCENDANTS

The nature of every individual on the planet is composed of the rich variety of zodiac signs and planetary positions that were present at the time of their birth. Your Sun sign, which in your case is Cancer, is one of the many factors when it comes to assessing the unique person you are. Probably the most important consideration, other than your Sun sign, is to establish the zodiac sign that was rising over the eastern horizon at the time that you were born. This is your Ascending or Rising sign. Most popular astrology fails to take account of the Ascendant, and yet its importance remains with you from the very moment of your birth, through every day of your life. The Ascendant is evident in the way you approach the world, and so, when meeting a person for the first time, it is this astrological influence that you are most likely to notice first. Our Ascending sign essentially represents what we appear to be, while the Sun sign is what we feel inside ourselves.

The Ascendant also has the potential for modifying our overall nature. For example, if you were born at a time of day when Cancer was passing over the eastern horizon (this would be around the time of dawn) then you would be classed as a double Cancerian. As such, you would typify this zodiac sign, both internally and in your dealings with others. However, if your Ascendant sign turned out to be a Fire sign, such as Aries, there would be a profound alteration of nature, away from the expected qualities of Cancer.

One of the reasons why popular astrology often ignores the Ascendant is that it has always been rather difficult to establish. Old Moore has found a way to make this possible by devising an easy-to-use table, which you will find on page 158 of this book. Using this, you can establish your Ascendant sign at a glance. You will need to know your rough time of birth, then it is simply a case of following the instructions.

For those readers who have no idea of their time of birth it might be worth allowing a good friend, or perhaps your partner, to read through the section that follows this introduction. Someone who deals with you on a regular basis may easily discover your Ascending sign, even though you could have some difficulty establishing it for yourself. A good understanding of this component of your nature is essential if you want to be aware of that 'other person' who is responsible for the way you make contact with the world at large. Your Sun sign, Ascendant sign, and the other pointers in this book will, together, allow you a far better understanding of what makes you tick as an individual. Peeling back the different layers of your astrological make-up can be an enlightening experience, and the Ascendant may represent one of the most important layers of all.

Cancer with Cancer Ascendant

You are one of the most warm and loving individuals that it is possible to know, and you carry a quiet dignity that few would fail to recognise. Getting on with things in your own steady way, you are, nevertheless, capable of great things, simply because you keep going. Even in the face of adversity your steady but relentless pace can be observed, and much of what you do is undertaken on behalf of those you love the most. On the other side of the coin you represent something of a mystery and it is also true that emotionally speaking you tend to be very highly charged. It doesn't take much to bring you to tears and you are inclined to have a special affection for the underdog, which on occasions can get you into a little trouble. Although it is your natural way to keep a low profile, you will speak out loudly if you think that anyone you care for is under attack, and yet you don't show the same tendency on your own behalf.

Rarely if ever out of control, you are the levelling influence everyone feels they need in their life, which is one of the reasons why you are so loved. Your quiet ways are accepted by the world, which is why some people will be astonished when you suddenly announce that you are about to travel overland to Asia. What a great puzzle you can be, but that is half the attraction.

Cancer with Leo Ascendant

This can be a very fortunate combination, for when seen at its best it brings all the concern and the natural caring qualities of Cancer, allied to the more dynamic and very brave face of Leo. Somehow there is a great deal of visible energy here, but it manifests itself in a way that always shows a concern for the world at large. No matter what charitable works are going on in your district it is likely that you will be involved in one way or another, and you relish the cut and thrust of life much more than the the retiring side of Cancer would seem to do. You are quite capable of walking alone and don't really need the company of others for large chunks of the average day. However, when you are in social situations you fare very well and can usually be observed with a smile on your face.

Conversationally speaking you have sound, considered opinions and often represent the voice of steady wisdom when faced with a situation that means arbitration. In fact you will often be put in this situation, and there is more than one politician and union representative who shares this undeniably powerful zodiac combination. Like all those associated with the sign of Cancer you love to travel and can make a meal out of your journeys with brave, intrepid Leo lending a hand in both the planning and the doing.

Cancer with Virgo Ascendant

What can this union of zodiac signs bring to the party that isn't there in either Cancer or Virgo alone? Well, quite a bit actually. Virgo can be very fussy on occasions and too careful for its own good. The presence of steady, serene Cancer alters the perspectives and allows a smoother, more flowing individual to greet the world. You are chatty and easy to know, and exhibit a combination of the practical skills of Virgo, together with the deep and penetrating insights that are typical of Cancer. This can make you appear to be very powerful and your insights are second to none. You are a born organiser and love to be where things are happening, even if you are only there to help make the sandwiches or to pour the tea. Invariably your role will be much greater but you don't seek personal acclaim and are a good team player on most occasions.

There is a quiet side to your nature and those who live with you will eventually get used to your need for solitude. This seems strange because Virgo is generally such a chatterbox and, taken on its own, is rarely quiet for long. In matters of love you show great affection and a sense of responsibility that makes you an ideal parent. It is sometimes the case, however, that you care rather more than you should be willing to show.

Cancer with Libra Ascendant

What an absolutely pleasant and approachable sort of person you are, and how much you have to offer. Like most people associated with the sign of Cancer, you give yourself freely to the world and will always be on hand if anyone is in trouble or needs the special touch you can bring to almost any problem. Behaving in this way is the biggest part of what you are and so people come to rely on you very heavily. Like Libra you can see both sides of any coin and you exhibit the Libran tendency to jump about from one foot to the other when it is necessary to make decisions relating to your own life. This is not usually the case when you are dealing with others, however, because the cooler and more detached qualities of Cancer will show through in these circumstances.

It would be fair to say that you do not deal with routines as well as Cancer alone might do and you need a degree of variety in your life. In your case this possibly comes in the form of travel, which can be distant and of long duration. It isn't unusual for people who have this zodiac combination to end up living abroad, though even this does little to prevent you from getting itchy feet from time to time. In relationships you show an original quality that keeps the relationship young, fresh and working well.

Cancer with Scorpio Ascendant

There are few more endearing zodiac combinations than this. Both signs are Watery in nature and show a desire to work on behalf of humanity as a whole. The world sees you as being genuinely caring, full of sympathy for anyone in trouble and always ready to lend a hand when it is needed. You are a loyal friend, a great supporter of the oppressed and a lover of home and family. In a work sense you are capable and command respect from your colleagues, even though this comes about courtesy of your quiet competence, and not as a result of anything that you might happen to say or do.

But we should not get too carried away with external factors, or the way that others see you. Inside you are a boiling pool of emotion. You feel more strongly, love more deeply and hurt more fully than any other combination of the Water signs. Even those who think that they know you really well would get a shock if they could take a stroll around the deeper recesses of your mind. Although these facts are true, they may be rather beside the point because the truth of your passion, commitment and deep convictions may only surface fully half a dozen times in your life. The fact is that you are a very private person at heart and you don't know how to be any other way.

Cancer with Sagittarius Ascendant

You have far more drive, enthusiasm and get-up-and-go than would seem to be the case for Cancer when taken alone, but all of this is tempered with a certain quiet compassion that probably makes you the best sort of Sagittarian too. It's true that you don't like to be on your own or to retire into your shell quite as much as the Crab usually does, though there are, even in your case, occasions when this is going to be necessary. Absolute concentration can sometimes be a problem to you, though this is hardly likely to be the case when you are dealing with matters relating to your home or family, both of which reign supreme in your thinking. Always loving and kind, you are a social animal and enjoy being out there in the real world, expressing the deeper opinions of Cancer much more readily than would often be the case with other combinations relating to the sign of the Crab.

Personality is not lacking, and you tend to be very popular, not least because you are the fountain of good and practical advice. You want to get things done, and retain a practical approach to most situations which is the envy of many of the people you meet. As a parent you are second to none, combining common sense, dignity and a sensible approach. To balance this you stay young enough to understand children.

Cancer with Capricorn Ascendant

The single most important factor here is the practical ability to get things done and to see any task, professional or personal, through to the end. Since half this combination is Cancer, that also means expounding much of your energy on behalf of others. There isn't a charity in the world that would fail to recognise what a potent combination this is when it comes to the very concrete side of offering help and assistance. Many of your ideas hold water and you don't set off on abortive journeys of any kind, simply because you tend to get the ground rules fixed in your mind first.

On a more personal level you can be rather hard to get to know, because both these signs have a deep quality and a tendency to keep things in the dark. The mystery may only serve to encourage people to try and get to know you better. As a result you could attract a host of admirers, many of whom would wish to form romantic attachments. This may prove to be irrelevant, however, because once you give your heart, you tend to be loyal and would only change your mind if you were pushed into doing so. Prolonged periods of inactivity don't do you any good and it is sensible for you to keep on the move, even though your progress in life is measured and very steady.

Cancer with Aquarius Ascendant

The truly original spark, for which the sign of Aquarius is famed, can only enhance the caring qualities of Cancer, and is also inclined to bring the Crab out of its shell to a much greater extent than would be the case with certain other zodiac combinations. Aquarius is a party animal and never arrives without something interesting to say, which is doubly so when the reservoir of emotion and consideration that is Cancer is feeding the tap. Your nature can be rather confusing, even for you to deal with, but you are inspirational, bright, charming and definitely fun to be around.

The Cancer element in your nature means that you care about your home and the people to whom you are related. You are also a good and loyal friend, who would keep attachments for much longer than could be expected for Aquarius alone. You love to travel and can be expected to make many journeys to far-off places during your life. Some attention will have to be paid to your health because you are capable of burning up masses of nervous energy, often without getting the periods of rest and contemplation that are essential to the deeper qualities of the sign of Cancer. Nevertheless you have determination, resilience and a refreshing attitude that lifts the spirits of the people in your vicinity.

Cancer with Pisces Ascendant

A deep, double Water-sign combination, this one, and it might serve to make you a very misunderstood, though undoubtedly popular, individual. You are keen to make a good impression, probably too keen under certain circumstances, and you do everything you can to help others, even if you don't know them very well. It's true that you are deeply sensitive and quite easily brought to tears by the suffering of this most imperfect world that we inhabit. Fatigue can be a problem, though this is nullified to some extent by the fact that you can withdraw completely into the deep recesses of your own mind when it becomes necessary to do so.

You may not be the most gregarious person in the world, simply because it isn't easy for you to put your most important considerations into words. This is easier when you are in the company of people you know and trust, though even trust is a commodity that is difficult for you to find, particularly since you may have been hurt by being too willing to share your thoughts early in life. With age comes wisdom and maturity and the older you are, the better you will learn to handle this potent and demanding combination. You will never go short of either friends or would-be lovers, and may be one of the most magnetic types of both Cancer and Pisces.

Cancer with Aries Ascendant

The main problem that you experience in life shows itself as a direct result of the meshing of these two very different zodiac signs. At heart Aries needs to dominate, whereas Cancer shows a desire to nurture. All too often the result can be a protective arm that is so strong that nobody could possibly get out from under it. Lighten your own load, and that of those you care for, by being willing to sit back and watch others please themselves a little. You might think that you know best, and your heart is clearly in the right place, but try and realise what life can be like when someone is always on hand to tell you that they know better than you do.

But in a way this is a little severe, because you are fairly intuitive and your instincts will rarely lead you astray. Nobody could ask for a better partner or parent than you would be, though they might request a slightly less attentive one. In matters of work you are conscientious, and are probably best suited to a job that means sorting out the kind of mess that humanity is so good at creating. You probably spend your spare time untangling balls of wool, though you are quite sporting too and could even make the Olympics. Once there you would not win however, because you would be too concerned about all the other competitors!

Cancer with Taurus Ascendant

Your main aim in life seems to be to look after everyone and everything that you come across. From your deepest and most enduring human love, right down to the birds in the park, you really do care and you show that natural affection in many different ways. Your nature is sensitive and you are easily moved to tears, though this does not prevent you from pitching in and doing practical things to assist at just about any level. There is a danger that you could stifle those same people whom you set out to assist, and people with this zodiac combination are often unwilling, or unable, to allow their children to grow and leave the nest. More time spent considering what suits you would be no bad thing, but the problem is that you find it almost impossible to imagine any situation that doesn't involve your most basic need, which is to nurture.

You appear not to possess a selfish streak, though it sometimes turns out that in being certain that you understand the needs of the world, you are nevertheless treading on their toes. This eventual realisation can be very painful, but it isn't a stick with which you should beat yourself because at heart you are one of the kindest people imaginable. Your sense of fair play means that you are a quiet social reformer at heart.

Cancer with Gemini Ascendant

Many astrologers would say that this is a happy combination because some of the more flighty qualities of Gemini are somewhat modified by the steady influence of Cancer the Crab. To all intents and purposes you show the friendly and gregarious qualities of Gemini, but there is a thoughtful and even sometimes a serious quality that would not be present in Gemini when taken alone. Looking after people is high on your list of priorities and you do this most of the time. This is made possible because you have greater staying power than Gemini is usually said to possess and you can easily see fairly complicated situations through to their conclusion without becoming bored on the way.

The chances are that you will have many friends and that these people show great concern for your well-being, because you choose them carefully and show them a great deal of consideration. However, you will still be on the receiving end of gossip on occasions, and need to treat such situations with a healthy pinch of salt. Like all part-Geminis your nervous system is not as strong as you would wish to believe and family pressures in particular can put great strain on you. Activities of all kinds take your fancy and many people with this combination are attracted to sailing or wind surfing.

THE MOON AND THE PART IT PLAYS IN YOUR LIFE

In astrology the Moon is probably the single most important heavenly body after the Sun. Its unique position, as partner to the Earth on its journey around the solar system, means that the Moon appears to pass through the signs of the zodiac extremely quickly. The zodiac position of the Moon at the time of your birth plays a great part in personal character and is especially significant in the build-up of your emotional nature.

Sun Moon Cycles

The first lunar cycle deals with the part the position of the Moon plays relative to your Sun sign. I have made the fluctuations of this pattern easy for you to understand by means of a simple cyclic graph. It appears on the first page of each 'Your Month At A Glance', under the title 'Highs and Lows'. The graph displays the lunar cycle and you will soon learn to understand how its movements have a bearing on your level of energy and your abilities.

Your Own Moon Sign

Discovering the position of the Moon at the time of your birth has always been notoriously difficult because tracking the complex zodiac positions of the Moon is not easy. This process has been reduced to three simple stages with Old Moore's unique Lunar Tables. A breakdown of the Moon's zodiac positions can be found from page 25 onwards, so that once you know what your Moon Sign is, you can see what part this plays in the overall build-up of your personal character.

If you follow the instructions on the next page you will soon be able to work out exactly what zodiac sign the Moon occupied on the day that you were born and you can then go on to compare the reading for this position with those of your Sun sign and your Ascendant. It is partly the comparison between these three important positions that goes towards making you the unique individual you are.

HOW TO DISCOVER YOUR MOON SIGN

This is a three-stage process. You may need a pen and a piece of paper but if you follow the instructions below the process should only take a minute or so.

STAGE 1 First of all you need to know the Moon Age at the time of your birth. If you look at Moon Table 1, on page 23, you will find all the years between 1909 and 2007 down the left side. Find the year of your birth and then trace across to the right to the month of your birth. Where the two intersect you will find a number. This is the date of the New Moon in the month that you were born. You now need to count forward the number of days between the New Moon and your own birthday. For example, if the New Moon in the month of your birth was shown as being the 6th and you were born on the 20th, your Moon Age Day would be 14. If the New Moon in the month of your birth came after your birthday, you need to count forward from the New Moon in the previous month. Whatever the result, jot this number down so that you do not forget it.

STAGE 2 Take a look at Moon Table 2 on page 24. Down the left hand column look for the date of your birth. Now trace across to the month of your birth. Where the two meet you will find a letter. Copy this letter down alongside your Moon Age Day.

STAGE 3 Moon Table 3 on page 24 will supply you with the zodiac sign the Moon occupied on the day of your birth. Look for your Moon Age Day down the left hand column and then for the letter you found in Stage 2. Where the two converge you will find a zodiac sign and this is the sign occupied by the Moon on the day that you were born.

Your Zodiac Moon Sign Explained

You will find a profile of all zodiac Moon Signs on pages 25 to 28, showing in yet another way how astrology helps to make you into the individual that you are. In each daily entry of the Astral Diary you can find the zodiac position of the Moon for every day of the year. This also allows you to discover your lunar birthdays. Since the Moon passes through all the signs of the zodiac in about a month, you can expect something like twelve lunar birthdays each year. At these times you are likely to be emotionally steady and able to make the sort of decisions that have real, lasting value.

MOON TABLE 1

YEAR	MAY	JUN	JUL	YEAR	MAY	JUN	JUL	YEAR	MAY	JUN	JUL
1909	19	17	17	1942	15	13	13	1975	11	9	9
1910	9	7	6	1943	4	2	2	1976	29	27	27
1911	28	26	25	1944	22	20	20	1977	18	16	16
1912	17	16	15	1945	11	10	9	1978	7	5	5
1913	5	4	3	1946	1/30	29	28	1979	26	24	24
1914	24	23	22	1947	19	18	17	1980	14	13	12
1915	13	12	11	1948	9	7	6	1981	4	2	1/31
1916	2	1/30	30	1949	27	26	25	1982	21	21	20
1917	20	19	18	1950	17	15	15	1983	12	11	10
1918	10	8	8	1951	6	4	4	1984	1/30	29	28
1919	29	27	27	1952	23	22	22	1985	19	18	17
1920	18	16	15	1953	13	11	11	1986	8	7	7
1921	7	6	5	1954	2	1/30	29	1987	27	26	25
1922	26	25	24	1955	21	20	19	1988	15	14	13
1923	15	14	14	1956	10	8	8	1989	5	3	3
1924	3	2	2/31	1957	29	27	27	1990	24	22	22
1925	22	21	20	1958	18	17	16	1991	13	11	11
1926	11	10	9	1959	7	6	6	1992	2	1/30	29
1927	2/31	29	28	1960	26	24	24	1993	21	19	19
1928	19	18	17	1961	14	13	12	1994	10	8	8
1929	9	7	6	1962	4	2	1/31	1995	29	27	27
1930	28	26	25	1963	23	21	20	1996	18	17	15
1931	17	16	15	1964	11	10	9	1997	6	5	4
1932	5	4	3	1965	1/30	29	28	1998	25	24	23
1933	24	23	22	1966	19	18	17	1999	15	13	13
1934	13	12	11	1967	8	7	7	2000	4	2	1/31
1935	2	1/30	30	1968	27	26	25	2001	23	21	20
1936	20	19	18	1969	15	14	13	2002	12	10	9
1937	10	8	8	1970	6	4	4	2003	1/30	29	28
1938	29	27	27	1971	24	22	22	2004	18	16	16
1939	19	17	16	1972	13	11	11	2005	8	6	6
1940	7	6	5	1973	2	1/30	29	2006	27	26	25
1941	26	24	24	1974	21	20	19	2007	17	15	15

TABLE 2

DAY	JUN	JUL
1	O	R
2	P	R
3	P	S
4	P	S
5	P	S
6	P	S
7	P	S
8	P	S
9	P	S
10	P	S
11	P	S
12	Q	S
13	Q	T
14	Q	T
15	Q	T
16	Q	T
17	Q	T
18	Q	T
19	Q	T
20	Q	T
21	Q	T
22	R	T
23	R	T
24	R	U
25	R	U
26	R	U
27	R	U
28	R	U
29	R	U
30	R	U
31	–	U

MOON TABLE 3

M/D	O	P	Q	R	S	T	U
0	GE	GE	CA	CA	CA	LE	LE
1	GE	CA	CA	CA	LE	LE	LE
2	CA	CA	CA	LE	LE	LE	VI
3	CA	CA	LE	LE	LE	VI	VI
4	LE	LE	LE	LE	VI	VI	LI
5	LE	LE	VI	VI	VI	LI	LI
6	VI	VI	VI	VI	LI	LI	LI
7	VI	VI	LI	LI	LI	LI	SC
8	VI	VI	LI	LI	LI	SC	SC
9	LI	LI	SC	SC	SC	SC	SA
10	LI	LI	SC	SC	SC	SA	SA
11	SC	SC	SC	SA	SA	SA	CP
12	SC	SC	SA	SA	SA	SA	CP
13	SC	SA	SA	SA	SA	CP	CP
14	SA	SA	SA	CP	CP	CP	AQ
15	SA	SA	CP	CP	CP	AQ	AQ
16	CP	CP	CP	AQ	AQ	AQ	AQ
17	CP	CP	CP	AQ	AQ	AQ	PI
18	CP	CP	AQ	AQ	AQ	PI	PI
19	AQ	AQ	AQ	PI	PI	PI	PI
20	AQ	AQ	PI	PI	PI	AR	AR
21	AQ	PI	PI	PI	AR	AR	AR
22	PI	PI	PI	AR	AR	AR	TA
23	PI	PI	AR	AR	AR	TA	TA
24	PI	AR	AR	AR	TA	TA	TA
25	AR	AR	TA	TA	TA	GE	GE
26	AR	TA	TA	TA	GE	GE	GE
27	TA	TA	TA	GE	GE	GE	CA
28	TA	TA	GE	GE	GE	CA	CA
29	TA	GE	GE	GE	CA	CA	CA

AR = Aries, TA = Taurus, GE = Gemini, CA = Cancer, LE = Leo, VI = Virgo, LI = Libra, SC = Scorpio, SA = Sagittarius, CP = Capricorn, AQ = Aquarius, PI = Pisces

MOON SIGNS

Moon in Aries

You have a strong imagination, courage, determination and a desire to do things in your own way and forge your own path through life.

Originality is a key attribute; you are seldom stuck for ideas although your mind is changeable and you could take the time to focus on individual tasks. Often quick-tempered, you take orders from few people and live life at a fast pace. Avoid health problems by taking regular time out for rest and relaxation.

Emotionally, it is important that you talk to those you are closest to and work out your true feelings. Once you discover that people are there to help, there is less necessity for you to do everything yourself.

Moon in Taurus

The Moon in Taurus gives you a courteous and friendly manner, which means you are likely to have many friends.

The good things in life mean a lot to you, as Taurus is an Earth sign that delights in experiences which please the senses. Hence you are probably a lover of good food and drink, which may in turn mean you need to keep an eye on the bathroom scales, especially as looking good is also important to you.

Emotionally you are fairly stable and you stick by your own standards. Taureans do not respond well to change. Intuition also plays an important part in your life.

Moon in Gemini

You have a warm-hearted character, sympathetic and eager to help others. At times reserved, you can also be articulate and chatty: this is part of the paradox of Gemini, which always brings duplicity to the nature. You are interested in current affairs, have a good intellect, and are good company and likely to have many friends. Most of your friends have a high opinion of you and would be ready to defend you should the need arise. However, this is usually unnecessary, as you are quite capable of defending yourself in any verbal confrontation.

Travel is important to your inquisitive mind and you find intellectual stimulus in mixing with people from different cultures. You also gain much from reading, writing and the arts but you do need plenty of rest and relaxation in order to avoid fatigue.

Moon in Cancer

The Moon in Cancer at the time of birth is a fortunate position as Cancer is the Moon's natural home. This means that the qualities of compassion and understanding given by the Moon are especially enhanced in your nature, and you are friendly and sociable and cope well with emotional pressures. You cherish home and family life, and happily do the domestic tasks. Your surroundings are important to you and you hate squalor and filth. You are likely to have a love of music and poetry.

Your basic character, although at times changeable like the Moon itself, depends on symmetry. You aim to make your surroundings comfortable and harmonious, for yourself and those close to you.

Moon in Leo

The best qualities of the Moon and Leo come together to make you warm-hearted, fair, ambitious and self-confident. With good organisational abilities, you invariably rise to a position of responsibility in your chosen career. This is fortunate as you don't enjoy being an 'also-ran' and would rather be an important part of a small organisation than a menial in a large one.

You should be lucky in love, and happy, provided you put in the effort to make a comfortable home for yourself and those close to you. It is likely that you will have a love of pleasure, sport, music and literature. Life brings you many rewards, most of them as a direct result of your own efforts, although you may be luckier than average and ready to make the best of any situation.

Moon in Virgo

You are endowed with good mental abilities and a keen receptive memory, but you are never ostentatious or pretentious. Naturally quite reserved, you still have many friends, especially of the opposite sex. Marital relationships must be discussed carefully and worked at so that they remain harmonious, as personal attachments can be a problem if you do not give them your full attention.

Talented and persevering, you possess artistic qualities and are a good homemaker. Earning your honours through genuine merit, you work long and hard towards your objectives but show little pride in your achievements. Many short journeys will be undertaken in your life.

Moon in Libra

With the Moon in Libra you are naturally popular and make friends easily. People like you, probably more than you realise, you bring fun to a party and are a natural diplomat. For all its good points, Libra is not the most stable of astrological signs and, as a result, your emotions can be a little unstable too. Therefore, although the Moon in Libra is said to be good for love and marriage, your Sun sign and Rising sign will have an important effect on your emotional and loving qualities.

You must remember to relate to others in your decision-making. Co-operation is crucial because Libra represents the 'balance' of life that can only be achieved through harmonious relationships. Conformity is not easy for you because Libra, an Air sign, likes its independence.

Moon in Scorpio

Some people might call you pushy. In fact, all you really want to do is to live life to the full and protect yourself and your family from the pressures of life. Take care to avoid giving the impression of being sarcastic or impulsive and use your energies wisely and constructively.

You have great courage and you invariably achieve your goals by force of personality and sheer effort. You are fond of mystery and are good at predicting the outcome of situations and events. Travel experiences can be beneficial to you.

You may experience problems if you do not take time to examine your motives in a relationship, and also if you allow jealousy, always a feature of Scorpio, to cloud your judgement.

Moon in Sagittarius

The Moon in Sagittarius helps to make you a generous individual with humanitarian qualities and a kind heart. Restlessness may be intrinsic as your mind is seldom still. Perhaps because of this, you have a need for change that could lead you to several major moves during your adult life. You are not afraid to stand your ground when you know your judgement is right, you speak directly and have good intuition.

At work you are quick, efficient and versatile and so you make an ideal employee. You need work to be intellectually demanding and do not enjoy tedious routines.

In relationships, you anger quickly if faced with stupidity or deception, though you are just as quick to forgive and forget. Emotionally, there are times when your heart rules your head.

Moon in Capricorn

The Moon in Capricorn makes you popular and likely to come into the public eye in some way. The watery Moon is not entirely comfortable in the Earth sign of Capricorn and this may lead to some difficulties in the early years of life. An initial lack of creative ability and indecision must be overcome before the true qualities of patience and perseverance inherent in Capricorn can show through.

You have good administrative ability and are a capable worker, and if you are careful you can accumulate wealth. But you must be cautious and take professional advice in partnerships, as you are open to deception. You may be interested in social or welfare work, which suit your organisational skills and sympathy for others.

Moon in Aquarius

The Moon in Aquarius makes you an active and agreeable person with a friendly, easy-going nature. Sympathetic to the needs of others, you flourish in a laid-back atmosphere. You are broad-minded, fair and open to suggestion, although sometimes you have an unconventional quality which others can find hard to understand.

You are interested in the strange and curious, and in old articles and places. You enjoy trips to these places and gain much from them. Political, scientific and educational work interests you and you might choose a career in science or technology.

Money-wise, you make gains through innovation and concentration and Lunar Aquarians often tackle more than one job at a time. In love you are kind and honest.

Moon in Pisces

You have a kind, sympathetic nature, somewhat retiring at times, but you always take account of others' feelings and help when you can.

Personal relationships may be problematic, but as life goes on you can learn from your experiences and develop a better understanding of yourself and the world around you.

You have a fondness for travel, appreciate beauty and harmony and hate disorder and strife. You may be fond of literature and would make a good writer or speaker yourself. You have a creative imagination and may come across as an incurable romantic. You have strong intuition, maybe bordering on a mediumistic quality, which sets you apart from the mass. You may not be rich in cash terms, but your personal gifts are worth more than gold.

CANCER IN LOVE

Discover how compatible in love you are with people from the same and other signs of the zodiac. Five stars equals a match made in heaven!

Cancer meets Cancer

This match will work because the couple share a mutual understanding. Cancerians are very kind people who also respond well to kindness from others, so a double Cancer match can almost turn into a mutual appreciation society! But this will not lead to selfish hedonism, as the Crab takes in order to give more. There is an impressive physical, emotional and spiritual meeting of minds, which will lead to a successful and inspiring pairing in its own low-key and deeply sensitive way. Star rating: *****

Cancer meets Leo

This relationship will usually be directed by Leo more towards its own needs than Cancer's. However, the Crab will willingly play second fiddle to more progressive and bossy types as it is deeply emotional and naturally supportive. Leo is bright, caring, magnanimous and protective and so, as long as it isn't over-assertive, this could be a good match. On the surface, Cancer appears the more conventional of the two, but Leo will discover, to its delight, that it can be unusual and quirky. Star rating: ****

Cancer meets Virgo

This match has little chance of success, for fairly simple reasons: Cancer's generous affection will be submerged by the Virgoan depths, not because Virgo is uncaring but because it expresses itself so differently. As both signs are naturally quiet, things might become a bit boring. They would be mutually supportive, possibly financially successful and have a very tidy house, but they won't share much sparkle, enthusiasm, risk-taking or passion. If this pair were stranded on a desert island, they might live at different ends of it. Star rating: **

Cancer meets Libra

Almost anyone can get on with Libra, which is one of the most adaptable signs of them all. But being adaptable does not always lead to fulfilment, and a successful match here will require a quiet Libran and a slightly more progressive Cancerian than the norm. Both signs are pleasant, polite and like domestic order, but Libra may find Cancer too emotional and perhaps lacking in vibrancy, while Libra, on the other hand, may be a little too flighty for steady Cancer. Star rating: ***

Cancer meets Scorpio

This match is potentially a great success, a fact which is often a mystery to astrologers. Some feel it is due to the compatibility of the Water element, but it could also come from a mixture of similarity and difference in the personalities. Scorpio is partly ruled by Mars, which gives it a deep, passionate, dominant and powerful side. Cancerians generally like and respect this amalgam, and recognise something there that they would like to adopt themselves. On the other side of the coin, Scorpio needs love and emotional security which Cancer offers generously. Star rating: *****

Cancer meets Sagittarius

Although probably not an immediate success, there is hope for this couple. It's hard to see how this pair could get together, because they have few mutual interests. Sagittarius is always on the go, loves a hectic social life and dances the night away. Cancer prefers the cinema or a concert. But, having met, Cancer will appreciate the Archer's happy and cheerful nature, while Sagittarius finds Cancer alluring and intriguing and, as the saying goes, opposites attract. A long-term relationship would focus on commitment to family, with Cancer leading this area. Star rating: ***

Cancer meets Capricorn

Just about the only thing this pair have in common is the fact that both signs begin with 'Ca'! Some signs of the zodiac are instigators and some are reactors, and both the Crab and the Goat are reactors. Consequently, they both need incentives from their partners but won't find it in each other and, with neither side taking the initiative, there's a spark missing. Cancer and Capricorn do think alike in some ways and so, if they can find their spark or common purpose, they can be as happy as anyone. It's just rather unlikely. Star rating: **

Cancer meets Aquarius

Cancer is often attracted to Aquarius and, as Aquarius is automatically on the side of anyone who fancies it, so there is the potential for something good here. Cancer loves Aquarius' devil-may-care approach to life, but also recognises and seeks to strengthen the basic lack of self-confidence that all Air signs try so hard to keep secret. Both signs are natural travellers and are quite adventurous. Their family life would be unusual, even peculiar, but friends would recognise a caring, sharing household with many different interests shared by people genuinely in love. Star rating: ***

Cancer meets Pisces

This is likely to be a very successful match. Cancer and Pisces are both Water signs, and are both deep, sensitive and very caring. Pisces loves deeply, and Cancer wants to be loved. There will be few fireworks here, and a very quiet house. But that doesn't mean that either love or action is lacking – the latter of which is just behind closed doors. Family and children are important to both signs and both are prepared to work hard, but Pisces is the more restless of the two and needs the support and security that Cancer offers. Star rating: ★★★★★

Cancer meets Aries

A potentially one-sided pairing, it often appears that the Cancerian is brow-beaten by the far more dominant Arian. So much depends on the patience of the Cancerian individual, because if good psychology is present – who knows? But beware, Aries, you may find your partner too passive, and constantly having to take the lead can be wearing – even for you. A prolonged trial period would be advantageous, as the match could easily go either way. When it does work, though, this relationship is usually contented. Star rating: ★★★

Cancer meets Taurus

This pair will have the tidiest house in the street – every stick of furniture in place, and no errant blade of grass daring to spoil the lawn. But things inside the relationship might not be quite so ship-shape as both signs need, but don't offer, encouragement. There's plenty of affection, but few incentives for mutual progress. This might not prevent material success, but an enduring relationship isn't based on money alone. Passion is essential, and both parties need to realise and aim for that. Star rating: ★★

Cancer meets Gemini

This is often a very good match. Cancer is a very caring sign and quite adaptable. Geminis are untidy, have butterfly minds and are usually full of a thousand different schemes which Cancerians take in their stride and even relish. They can often be the 'wind beneath the wings' of their Gemini partners. In return, Gemini can eradicate some of the Cancerian emotional insecurity and will be more likely to be faithful in thought, word and deed to Cancer than to almost any other sign. Star rating: ★★★★

VENUS:
THE PLANET OF LOVE

If you look up at the sky around sunset or sunrise you will often see Venus in close attendance to the Sun. It is arguably one of the most beautiful sights of all and there is little wonder that historically it became associated with the goddess of love. But although Venus does play an important part in the way you view love and in the way others see you romantically, this is only one of the spheres of influence that it enjoys in your overall character.

Venus has a part to play in the more cultured side of your life and has much to do with your appreciation of art, literature, music and general creativity. Even the way you look is responsive to the part of the zodiac that Venus occupied at the start of your life, though this fact is also down to your Sun sign and Ascending sign. If, at the time you were born, Venus occupied one of the more gregarious zodiac signs, you will be more likely to wear your heart on your sleeve, as well as to be more attracted to entertainment, social gatherings and good company. If on the other hand Venus occupied a quiet zodiac sign at the time of your birth, you would tend to be more retiring and less willing to shine in public situations.

It's good to know what part the planet Venus plays in your life for it can have a great bearing on the way you appear to the rest of the world and since we all have to mix with others, you can learn to make the very best of what Venus has to offer you.

One of the great complications in the past has always been trying to establish exactly what zodiac position Venus enjoyed when you were born because the planet is notoriously difficult to track. However, I have solved that problem by creating a table that is exclusive to your Sun sign, which you will find on the following page.

Establishing your Venus sign could not be easier. Just look up the year of your birth on the page opposite and you will see a sign of the zodiac. This was the sign that Venus occupied in the period covered by your sign in that year. If Venus occupied more than one sign during the period, this is indicated by the date on which the sign changed, and the name of the new sign. For instance, if you were born in 1950, Venus was in Taurus until the 27th June, after which time it was in Gemini. If you were born before 27th June your Venus sign is Taurus, if you were born on or after 27th June, your Venus sign is Gemini. Once you have established the position of Venus at the time of your birth, you can then look in the pages which follow to see how this has a bearing on your life as a whole.

1909 CANCER / 5.7 LEO	1958 TAURUS / 26.6 GEMINI
1910 TAURUS / 30.6 GEMINI	1959 LEO / 9.7 VIRGO
1911 LEO / 7.7 VIRGO	1960 CANCER / 16.7 LEO
1912 GEMINI / 25.6 CANCER /	1961 TAURUS / 7.7 GEMINI
19.7 LEO	1962 LEO / 13.7 VIRGO
1913 TAURUS / 8.7 GEMINI	1963 GEMINI / 8.7 CANCER
1914 LEO / 16.7 VIRGO	1964 CANCER / 22.6 GEMINI
1915 GEMINI / 11.7 CANCER	1965 CANCER / 1.7 LEO
1916 CANCER	1966 TAURUS / 26.6 GEMINI
1917 CANCER / 5.7 LEO	1967 LEO / 10.7 VIRGO
1918 TAURUS / 29.6 GEMINI	1968 CANCER / 16.7 LEO
1919 LEO / 8.7 VIRGO	1969 TAURUS / 6.7 GEMINI
1920 GEMINI / 25.6 CANCER /	1970 LEO / 13.7 VIRGO
18.7 LEO	1971 GEMINI / 7.7 CANCER
1921 TAURUS / 8.7 GEMINI	1972 CANCER / 22.6 GEMINI
1922 LEO / 15.7 VIRGO	1973 TAURUS / 30.6 LEO
1923 GEMINI / 10.7 CANCER	1974 TAURUS / 26.6 GEMINI /
1924 CANCER	22.7 CANCER
1925 CANCER / 4.7 LEO	1975 LEO / 10.7 VIRGO
1926 TAURUS / 28.6 GEMINI	1976 CANCER / 15.7 LEO
1927 LEO / 8.7 VIRGO	1977 TAURUS / 6.7 GEMINI
1928 GEMINI / 24.6 CANCER /	1978 LEO / 12.7 VIRGO
18.7 LEO	1979 GEMINI / 7.7 CANCER
1929 TAURUS / 8.7 GEMINI	1980 CANCER / 22.6 GEMINI
1930 LEO / 15.7 VIRGO	1981 CANCER / 30.6 LEO
1931 GEMINI / 10.7 CANCER	1982 TAURUS / 26.6 GEMINI /
1932 CANCER	21.7 CANCER
1933 CANCER / 4.7 LEO	1983 LEO / 10.7 VIRGO
1934 TAURUS / 27.6 GEMINI	1984 CANCER / 15.7 LEO
1935 LEO / 8.7 VIRGO	1985 TAURUS / 6.7 GEMINI
1936 GEMINI / 24.6 CANCER /	1986 LEO / 12.7 VIRGO
17.7 LEO	1987 GEMINI / 6.7 CANCER
1937 TAURUS / 8.7 GEMINI	1988 CANCER / 22.6 GEMINI
1938 LEO / 14.7 VIRGO	1989 CANCER / 29.6 LEO
1939 GEMINI / 9.7 CANCER	1990 TAURUS / 25.6 GEMINI /
1940 CANCER / 13.7 GEMINI	20.7 CANCER
1941 CANCER / 3.7 LEO	1991 LEO / 11.7 VIRGO
1942 TAURUS / 27.6 GEMINI	1992 CANCER / 14.7 LEO
1943 LEO / 9.7 VIRGO	1993 TAURUS / 5.7 GEMINI
1944 GEMINI / 23.6 CANCER /	1994 LEO / 11.7 VIRGO
17.7 LEO	1995 GEMINI / 5.7 CANCER
1945 TAURUS / 7.7 GEMINI	1996 CANCER / 22.6 GEMINI
1946 LEO / 14.7 VIRGO	1997 CANCER / 29.6 LEO
1947 GEMINI / 9.7 CANCER	1998 TAURUS / 25.6 GEMINI /
1948 CANCER / 6.7 GEMINI	20.7 CANCER
1949 CANCER / 2.7 LEO	1999 LEO / 11.7 VIRGO
1950 TAURUS / 27.6 GEMINI	2000 CANCER / 14.7 LEO
1951 LEO / 9.7 VIRGO	2001 TAURUS / 5.7 GEMINI
1952 GEMINI / 23.6 CANCER /	2002 LEO / 11.7 VIRGO
17.7 LEO	2003 GEMINI / 5.7 CANCER
1953 TAURUS / 7.7 GEMINI	2004 CANCER / 22.6 GEMINI
1954 LEO / 13.7 VIRGO	2005 CANCER / 29.6 LEO
1955 GEMINI / 8.7 CANCER	2006 TAURUS / 25.6 GEMINI /
1956 CANCER / 29.6 GEMINI	20.7 CANCER
1957 CANCER / 1.7 LEO	2007 LEO / 11.7 VIRGO

VENUS THROUGH THE ZODIAC SIGNS

Venus in Aries

Amongst other things, the position of Venus in Aries indicates a fondness for travel, music and all creative pursuits. Your nature tends to be affectionate and you would try not to create confusion or difficulty for others if it could be avoided. Many people with this planetary position have a great love of the theatre, and mental stimulation is of the greatest importance. Early romantic attachments are common with Venus in Aries, so it is very important to establish a genuine sense of romantic continuity. Early marriage is not recommended, especially if it is based on sympathy. You may give your heart a little too readily on occasions.

Venus in Taurus

You are capable of very deep feelings and your emotions tend to last for a very long time. This makes you a trusting partner and lover, whose constancy is second to none. In life you are precise and careful and always try to do things the right way. Although this means an ordered life, which you are comfortable with, it can also lead you to be rather too fussy for your own good. Despite your pleasant nature, you are very fixed in your opinions and quite able to speak your mind. Others are attracted to you and historical astrologers always quoted this position of Venus as being very fortunate in terms of marriage. However, if you find yourself involved in a failed relationship, it could take you a long time to trust again.

Venus in Gemini

As with all associations related to Gemini, you tend to be quite versatile, anxious for change and intelligent in your dealings with the world at large. You may gain money from more than one source but you are equally good at spending it. There is an inference here that you are a good communicator, via either the written or the spoken word, and you love to be in the company of interesting people. Always on the look-out for culture, you may also be very fond of music, and love to indulge the curious and cultured side of your nature. In romance you tend to have more than one relationship and could find yourself associated with someone who has previously been a friend or even a distant relative.

Venus in Cancer

You often stay close to home because you are very fond of family and enjoy many of your most treasured moments when you are with those you love. Being naturally sympathetic, you will always do anything you can to support those around you, even people you hardly know at all. This charitable side of your nature is your most noticeable trait and is one of the reasons why others are naturally so fond of you. Being receptive and in some cases even psychic, you can see through to the soul of most of those with whom you come into contact. You may not commence too many romantic attachments but when you do give your heart, it tends to be unconditionally.

Venus in Leo

It must become quickly obvious to almost anyone you meet that you are kind, sympathetic and yet determined enough to stand up for anyone or anything that is truly important to you. Bright and sunny, you warm the world with your natural enthusiasm and would rarely do anything to hurt those around you, or at least not intentionally. In romance you are ardent and sincere, though some may find your style just a little overpowering. Gains come through your contacts with other people and this could be especially true with regard to romance, for love and money often come hand in hand for those who were born with Venus in Leo. People claim to understand you, though you are more complex than you seem.

Venus in Virgo

Your nature could well be fairly quiet no matter what your Sun sign might be, though this fact often manifests itself as an inner peace and would not prevent you from being basically sociable. Some delays and even the odd disappointment in love cannot be ruled out with this planetary position, though it's a fact that you will usually find the happiness you look for in the end. Catapulting yourself into romantic entanglements that you know to be rather ill-advised is not sensible, and it would be better to wait before you committed yourself exclusively to any one person. It is the essence of your nature to serve the world at large and through doing so it is possible that you will attract money at some stage in your life.

Venus in Libra

Venus is very comfortable in Libra and bestows upon those people who have this planetary position a particular sort of kindness that is easy to recognise. This is a very good position for all sorts of friendships and also for romantic attachments that usually bring much joy into your life. Few individuals with Venus in Libra would avoid marriage and since you are capable of great depths of love, it is likely that you will find a contented personal life. You like to mix with people of integrity and intelligence but don't take kindly to scruffy surroundings or work that means getting your hands too dirty. Careful speculation, good business dealings and money through marriage all seem fairly likely.

Venus in Scorpio

You are quite open and tend to spend money quite freely, even on those occasions when you don't have very much. Although your intentions are always good, there are times when you get yourself in to the odd scrape and this can be particularly true when it comes to romance, which you may come to late or from a rather unexpected direction. Certainly you have the power to be happy and to make others contented on the way, but you find the odd stumbling block on your journey through life and it could seem that you have to work harder than those around you. As a result of this, you gain a much deeper understanding of the true value of personal happiness than many people ever do, and are likely to achieve true contentment in the end.

Venus in Sagittarius

You are lighthearted, cheerful and always able to see the funny side of any situation. These facts enhance your popularity, which is especially high with members of the opposite sex. You should never have to look too far to find romantic interest in your life, though it is just possible that you might be too willing to commit yourself before you are certain that the person in question is right for you. Part of the problem here extends to other areas of life too. The fact is that you like variety in everything and so can tire of situations that fail to offer it. All the same, if you choose wisely and learn to understand your restless side, then great happiness can be yours.

Venus in Capricorn

The most notable trait that comes from Venus in this position is that it makes you trustworthy and able to take on all sorts of responsibilities in life. People are instinctively fond of you and love you all the more because you are always ready to help those who are in any form of need. Social and business popularity can be yours and there is a magnetic quality to your nature that is particularly attractive in a romantic sense. Anyone who wants a partner for a lover, a spouse and a good friend too would almost certainly look in your direction. Constancy is the hallmark of your nature and unfaithfulness would go right against the grain. You might sometimes be a little too trusting.

Venus in Aquarius

This location of Venus offers a fondness for travel and a desire to try out something new at every possible opportunity. You are extremely easy to get along with and tend to have many friends from varied backgrounds, classes and inclinations. You like to live a distinct sort of life and gain a great deal from moving about, both in a career sense and with regard to your home. It is not out of the question that you could form a romantic attachment to someone who comes from far away or be attracted to a person of a distinctly artistic and original nature. What you cannot stand is jealousy, for you have friends of both sexes and would want to keep things that way.

Venus in Pisces

The first thing people tend to notice about you is your wonderful, warm smile. Being very charitable by nature you will do anything to help others, even if you don't know them well. Much of your life may be spent sorting out situations for other people, but it is very important to feel that you are living for yourself too. In the main, you remain cheerful, and tend to be quite attractive to members of the opposite sex. Where romantic attachments are concerned, you could be drawn to people who are significantly older or younger than yourself or to someone with a unique career or point of view. It might be best for you to avoid marrying whilst you are still very young.

THE ASTRAL DIARY
HOW THE DIAGRAMS WORK

Through the picture diagrams in the Astral Diary I want to help you to plot your year. With them you can see where the positive and negative aspects will be found in each month. To make the most of them, all you have to do is remember where and when!

Let me show you how they work ...

THE MONTH AT A GLANCE

Just as there are twelve separate zodiac signs, so astrologers believe that each sign has twelve separate aspects to life. Each of the twelve segments relates to a different personal aspect. I list them all every month so that their meanings are always clear.

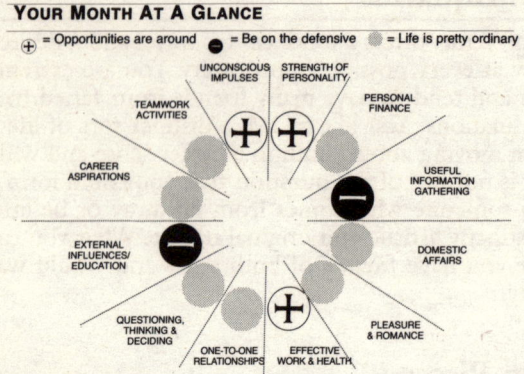

YOUR MONTH AT A GLANCE

⊕ = Opportunities are around ● = Be on the defensive ● = Life is pretty ordinary

UNCONSCIOUS IMPULSES
STRENGTH OF PERSONALITY
PERSONAL FINANCE
TEAMWORK ACTIVITIES
CAREER ASPIRATIONS
USEFUL INFORMATION GATHERING
EXTERNAL INFLUENCES/ EDUCATION
DOMESTIC AFFAIRS
QUESTIONING, THINKING & DECIDING
PLEASURE & ROMANCE
ONE-TO-ONE RELATIONSHIPS
EFFECTIVE WORK & HEALTH

I have designed this chart to show you how and when these twelve different aspects are being influenced throughout the year. When there is a shaded circle, nothing out of the ordinary is to be expected. However, when a circle turns white with a plus sign, the influence is positive. Where the circle is black with a minus sign, it is a negative.

YOUR ENERGY RHYTHM CHART

On the opposite page is a picture diagram in which I am linking your zodiac group to the rhythm of the Moon. In doing this I have calculated when you will be gaining strength from its influence and equally when you may be weakened by it.

If you think of yourself as being like the tides of the ocean then you may understand how your own energies must also rise and fall. And if you understand how it works and when it is working, then you can better organise your activities to achieve more and get things done more easily.

YOUR ENERGY RHYTHM CHART

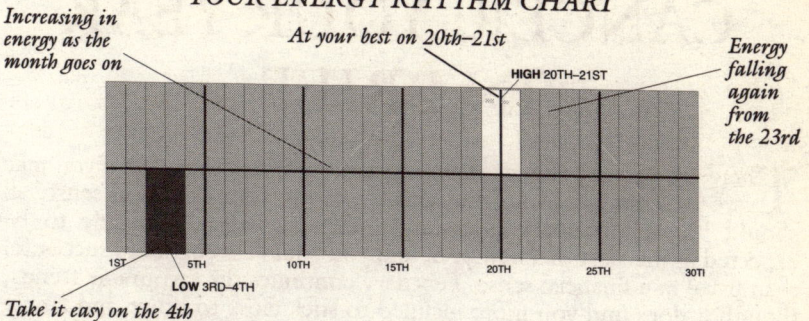

Increasing in energy as the month goes on

At your best on 20th–21st

HIGH 20TH–21ST

Energy falling again from the 23rd

1ST   5TH   10TH   15TH   20TH   25TH   30TI

LOW 3RD–4TH

Take it easy on the 4th

MOVING PICTURE SCREEN
Love, money, career and vitality measured every week

The diagram at the end of each week is designed to be informative and fun. The arrows move up and down the scale to give you an idea of the strength of your opportunities in each area. If LOVE stands at plus 4, then get out and put yourself about because things are going your way in romance! The further down the arrow goes, the weaker the opportunities. Do note that the diagram is an overall view of your astrological aspects and therefore reflects a trend which may not concur with every day in that cycle.

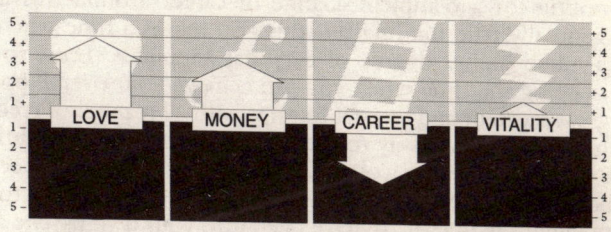

LOVE   MONEY   CAREER   VITALITY

AND FINALLY:

am ....

pm ....

The two lines that are left blank in each daily entry of the Astral Diary are for your own personal use. You may find them ideal for keeping a check on birthdays or appointments, though it could be an idea to make notes from the astrological trends and diagrams a few weeks in advance. Some of the lines are marked with a key, which indicates the working of astrological cycles in your life. Look out for them each week as they are the best days to take action or make decisions. The daily text tells you which area of your life to focus on.

☿ = Mercury is retrograde on that day.

CANCER: YOUR YEAR IN BRIEF

There are ups and downs at the beginning of this year, but if you take care to listen to advice and also to follow your common sense, all should be well. January offers new starts, which is probably to be expected at the start of a new year, and you could also be more successful than usual in a financial sense. February continues the favourable trends, though it does find you more inclined to stick close to home and family and maybe to be quieter generally.

With the early spring, March and April find you seeking to overturn obstacles that got in your path some time ago, and you might also be establishing contact with new individuals, as well as those who figured in your life previously. You won't get everything you want from a material point of view, but you should discover that most of the benefits of this period come free of charge in any case.

Come the month of May you will be seeking new horizons and enjoying the best of what early summer has to offer. Both May and June would be good for travel and for getting to grips with changes you want to make at work. It isn't out of the question that some Cancer subjects will be opting for a complete change of career around this time. The same is generally true for July but this also marks a time when you can achieve a much higher degree of personal happiness. Look to July and August as being the time when you can achieve your overall potential to a much greater extent and can get to grips with all manner of relationships.

As the summer gives way to the autumn you become slightly quieter and less inclined to push yourself as much as you have been doing. September could have financial highs, and together with October finds you more willing than ever to delve deep into your own psyche and those of people to whom you are somehow connected. Don't get hung up on details at this time.

The last two months of the year, November and December, should see you pushing forward solidly on most fronts, even if you have to take on board the wishes and plans of others in order to gain ground yourself. Avoid pitfalls that come from relying on the wrong people by simply using a mixture of that famous Cancerian intuition and common sense. The Christmas period looks especially heart-warming and cosy – but there is nothing particularly unusual about that as far as the Crab is concerned. Don't leave resolutions until the end of the month, but implement them somewhat earlier.

January 2007

YOUR MONTH AT A GLANCE

⊕ = Opportunities are around   ⊖ = Be on the defensive   ● = Life is pretty ordinary

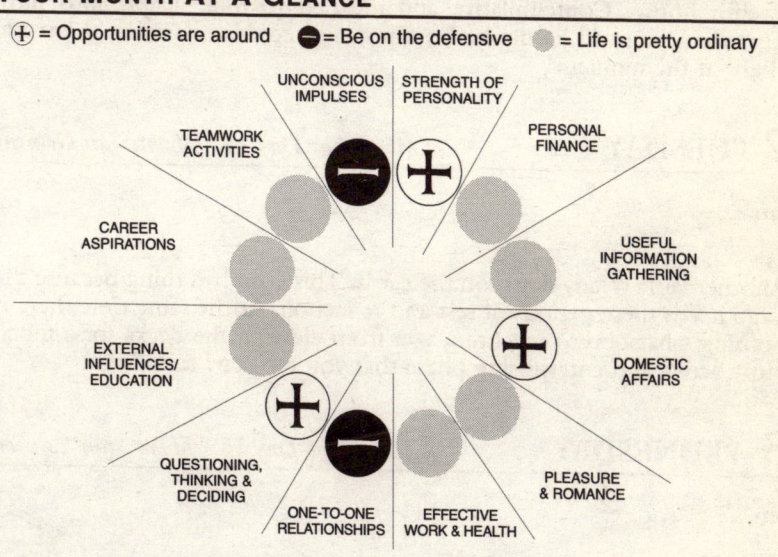

- UNCONSCIOUS IMPULSES
- STRENGTH OF PERSONALITY
- TEAMWORK ACTIVITIES
- PERSONAL FINANCE
- CAREER ASPIRATIONS
- USEFUL INFORMATION GATHERING
- EXTERNAL INFLUENCES/ EDUCATION
- DOMESTIC AFFAIRS
- QUESTIONING, THINKING & DECIDING
- PLEASURE & ROMANCE
- ONE-TO-ONE RELATIONSHIPS
- EFFECTIVE WORK & HEALTH

JANUARY HIGHS AND LOWS

Here I show you how the rhythms of the Moon will affect you this month. Like the tide, your energies and abilities will rise and fall with its pattern. When it is above the centre line, go for it, when it is below, you should be resting.

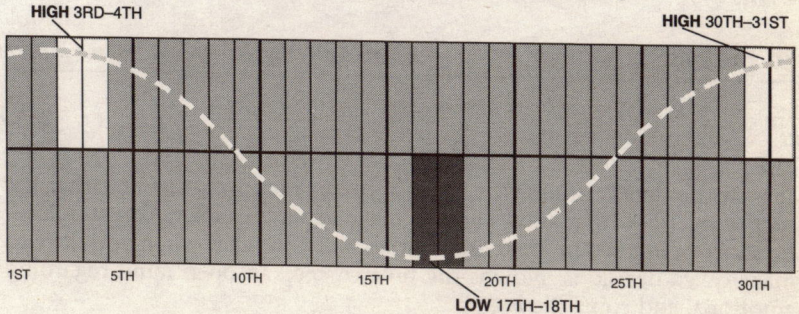

HIGH 3RD–4TH

HIGH 30TH–31ST

1ST   5TH   10TH   15TH   20TH   25TH   30TH

LOW 17TH–18TH

1 MONDAY
Moon Age Day 13   Moon Sign Gemini

am . . . .

pm . . . .
If things seem quite quiet as a new year gets going, you can put this fact down to the present position of the Moon, which occupies your solar twelfth house. Contemplative and inclined to look deeply into most situations, you will hardly be breaking any records or setting the world alight at the moment!

2 TUESDAY
Moon Age Day 14   Moon Sign Gemini

am . . . .

pm . . . .
Another fairly steady day is on the cards. This is no bad thing because the Crab needs these periods of rest and reflection. At the same time there is nothing whatsoever preventing you from clearing the decks for a much more active and enterprising phase that you can start tomorrow.

3 WEDNESDAY
Moon Age Day 15   Moon Sign Cancer

am . . . .

pm . . . .
The Moon now moves into your own zodiac sign, bringing that period that occurs each month and which is known as the lunar high. You know what you want and how to get it, whilst you can also be much more communicative and inclined to inspire others with your enthusiasm. This is a time to shine.

4 THURSDAY
Moon Age Day 16   Moon Sign Cancer

am . . . .

pm . . . .
It isn't the details of life that interest you at the moment but rather the sort of overview that allows you to make ground quickly. You shouldn't be short of important ideas and neither will you falter when you have to make quick decisions. Now is the time to keep an open mind regarding emotional and romantic issues.

5 FRIDAY

Moon Age Day 17   Moon Sign Leo

am . . . .

pm . . . .
Even if things slow somewhat today, you still have what it takes to make the best of impressions. It's possible that people have their eye on you at work and advancement soon is not out of the question. An impulsive streak is not far from the surface and in some ways you are quite untypical of the Cancerian nature.

6 SATURDAY

Moon Age Day 18   Moon Sign Leo

am . . . .

pm . . . .
There are new incentives about and you would be wise to do all you can to follow these up. Trends highlight your cultural side, and you may be much inspired by anything old or unusual. With a greater than average commitment to the community in which you live, this could be the time to get more involved.

7 SUNDAY

Moon Age Day 19   Moon Sign Virgo

am . . . .

pm . . . .
As often turns out to be the case, your primary concern today may well be towards family members and the needs they have of you. For the Crab this is a recurring theme and one you can't avoid. If younger people in particular are demanding your attention now, you can afford to do what you can to sort them out.

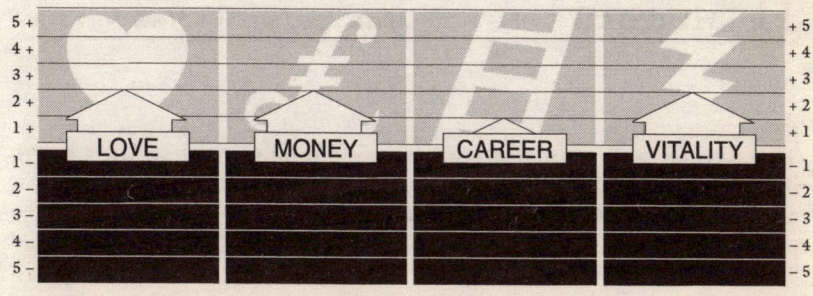

8 MONDAY
Moon Age Day 20   Moon Sign Virgo

am . . . .

pm . . . .
There are signs that your caring spirit is really on display at the moment – not that there is anything particularly unusual about that. It isn't just family members to whom you can give both your advice and your practical help but just about anyone you sense is in need. Be careful not to accidentally get on the wrong side of anyone's pride.

9 TUESDAY
Moon Age Day 21   Moon Sign Virgo

am . . . .

pm . . . .
This could be a more physically demanding day and one during which you can make sure your efforts start to pay small dividends. Be careful with cash for the moment because there could be bargains around later in the week. Social trends look good and you might be considering getting involved in some totally new activity.

10 WEDNESDAY
Moon Age Day 22   Moon Sign Libra

am . . . .

pm . . . .
Capitalise on new potential around now. You have scope to discover talents you didn't even know you had, and though you rarely have quite enough confidence in yourself you should find that you are getting on swimmingly. Even if not everyone is equally supportive at the moment, when it matters you can persuade others to come good.

11 THURSDAY
Moon Age Day 23   Moon Sign Libra

am . . . .

pm . . . .
There could well be a few complications around now and it's worth looking at all situations carefully before you react to them. You can show a warm face to the world at large and should be in your element when you are able to be of practical assistance. The chance of advancement at work cannot be ruled out under present trends.

12 FRIDAY

Moon Age Day 24   Moon Sign Scorpio

am . . . .

pm . . . .
You have what it takes to impress those who are in positions of authority at present and you can make the most of this situation by seeking something that is important to you. Having friends in high places is no bad thing, and it isn't in the least selfish to want to get on in life.

13 SATURDAY

Moon Age Day 25   Moon Sign Scorpio

am . . . .

pm . . . .
Professional aims and objectives could well be out of the window on a Saturday and so it is just as well that planetary trends right now favour a more relaxed approach to life, together with stronger social instincts. New friends are possible, together with a replay of a relationship from some time ago.

14 SUNDAY

Moon Age Day 26   Moon Sign Scorpio

am . . . .

pm . . . .
This ought to be another easy-going sort of day and one during which you are probably not exactly striving for anything. Getting to grips with a domestic issue that has been on your mind for some time could prove to be important, and you are in a position to make your home surroundings more comfortable in some way.

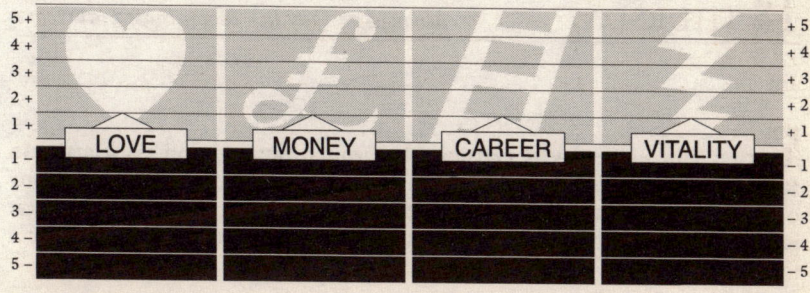

15 MONDAY   *Moon Age Day 27   Moon Sign Sagittarius*

am . . . .

pm . . . .
The start of a new working week encourages a vigorous approach and
offers a chance to seek assistance when you need it the most. Generally
speaking you should be jogging along quite nicely but there may be
people around who are difficult to weigh up. Your intuition remains
strong enough to get you through most situations.

16 TUESDAY   *Moon Age Day 28   Moon Sign Sagittarius*

am . . . .

pm . . . .
Emotional responses are highlighted, and you could be entering a more
romantic phase. It might appear that those to whom you are attached are
paying you far more attention than has been the case of late, but what is
probably happening is that there is a greater 'sharing' and a commonality
that could have been missing.

17 WEDNESDAY   *Moon Age Day 29   Moon Sign Capricorn*

am . . . .

pm . . . .
Things generally have potential to slow down for a day or two, and there
may not really be anything you can do about the situation. The Moon
has moved into your opposite zodiac sign of Capricorn, bringing the
lunar low, an event that happens on a monthly cycle. Go with the flow
and don't try to achieve too much.

18 THURSDAY   *Moon Age Day 0   Moon Sign Capricorn*

am . . . .

pm . . . .
Another lacklustre day is possible, but much depends on your attitude
and also on your aspirations. If you don't push too hard to achieve your
objectives, you won't be disappointed when you can't achieve them. This
is a time to stand on the riverbank of life and watch the water flow for a
few hours.

19 FRIDAY   *Moon Age Day 1   Moon Sign Aquarius*

am . . . .

pm . . . .
Things generally can be speeded up noticeably now the Moon has moved away from Capricorn. You have a chance to show yourself to be cheerful and willing to tackle almost anything. The fact that you are so flexible at the moment shouldn't be lost on people who are in a position to do you some good in the near future.

20 SATURDAY   *Moon Age Day 2   Moon Sign Aquarius*

am . . . .

pm . . . .
Look out for the chance to expand your social opportunities. You seem to be in the right frame of mind to stretch your interests and you can also afford to be more intrepid than might sometimes be the case. You may decide to plan now for a very special sort of holiday later in the year and consult loved ones about it.

21 SUNDAY   *Moon Age Day 3   Moon Sign Aquarius*

am . . . .

pm . . . .
Even if not everything goes exactly as you have planned, that shouldn't really matter as long as you react positively to changing times and circumstances. There are times when your nature prevents you from moving on, but this is probably not the case at the moment. In many ways it's off with the old and on with the new.

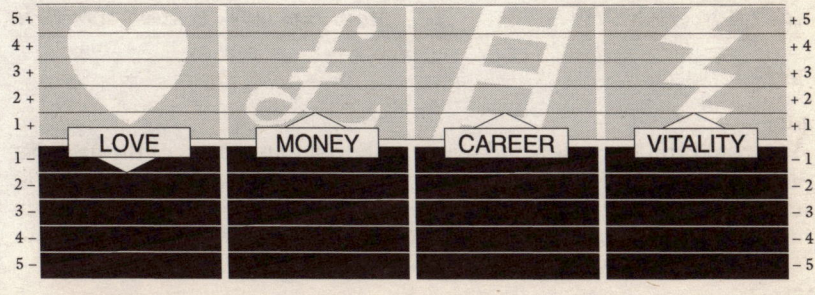

22 MONDAY

Moon Age Day 4   Moon Sign Pisces

am . . . .

pm . . . .
A little confusion is possible at the start of this week. Chances are that this comes about as a result of the behaviour of others, and it has little or nothing to do with you personally. All the same it might be up to you to sort things out and this diversion can be slightly frustrating. Its important to keep your patience with irritating types.

23 TUESDAY

Moon Age Day 5   Moon Sign Pisces

am . . . .

pm . . . .
Some Cancerians can now accomplish a number of changes to certain aspects of life. These are likely to be related to professional and practical matters and should have little bearing on your personal life. Once the cares of the day are dealt with you may well opt for a quiet evening, perhaps by your own fireside.

24 WEDNESDAY

Moon Age Day 6   Moon Sign Aries

am . . . .

pm . . . .
Trends assist you to broaden your horizons, and you could now have your sights set on a possible alteration to your working life that you will not have even suspected only a few days ago. To a great extent you are able to keep matters on the boil yourself because you now possess an innate desire for change.

25 THURSDAY

Moon Age Day 7   Moon Sign Aries

am . . . .

pm . . . .
You could still be restless and might wish to dump aspects of the past that are no longer any use to you. The problem for the Crab is that almost everything in life comes with emotional baggage and so it is often difficult to be ruthless. For you compromise is possible in just about everything, so beware of abandoning your plans.

26 FRIDAY
Moon Age Day 8   Moon Sign Taurus

am . . . .

pm . . . .
Restless and somewhat confused, the zodiac sign of Cancer needs time for reflection – but certainly not too much. There comes a moment when decisions have to be made and if you can't make up your own mind it might be useful to ask for an unbiased opinion from someone you trust.

27 SATURDAY
Moon Age Day 9   Moon Sign Taurus

am . . . .

pm . . . .
The weekend's trends encourage a stronger commitment to family members and a determination to get on top of any domestic jobs that have gone by the board during the working week. You have the ability to remain calmer than of late and to take most situations very much in your stride.

28 SUNDAY
Moon Age Day 10   Moon Sign Gemini

am . . . .

pm . . . .
What a good time this would be to start a completely new project. Even if it isn't anything major and the implications are not earth-shattering, it can be important all the same. Your intellectual curiosity is stimulated and there is more than a little of the detective about you under present astrological trends.

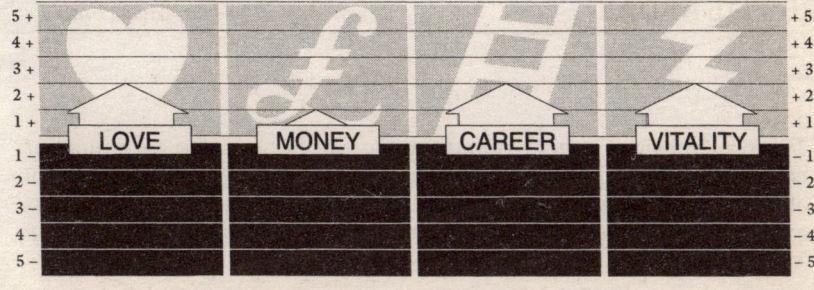

29 MONDAY
Moon Age Day 11   Moon Sign Gemini

am . . . .

pm . . . .
You can gain from better social co-operation and it ought to be quite easy
to mix business with pleasure at present. It is possible that you will be
slightly quieter than of late but you can put this down to the fact that the
Moon is presently in your solar twelfth house. You can make sure that
things change dramatically tomorrow.

30 TUESDAY
Moon Age Day 12   Moon Sign Cancer

am . . . .

pm . . . .
Along comes the time of the month during which the Moon occupies
your own zodiac sign. This is rightfully known as the lunar high and
especially so in your case, since the Moon is your ruling planet. You have
what it takes to stay busy and to keep up with anyone's thinking. This is
a time for action!

31 WEDNESDAY
Moon Age Day 13   Moon Sign Cancer

am . . . .

pm . . . .
The last day of January provides an opportunity to get ahead in just
about any way that proves to be possible. You can afford to jump at
chances without a second thought and to display the really inspirational
side of your nature. People love to have you around because you are
interesting, funny and yet very sharp.

1 THURSDAY
Moon Age Day 14   Moon Sign Leo

am . . . .

pm . . . .
This probably isn't your favoured time of year because you are a summer-
born person. Nevertheless you can make the most of anything that is on
offer and should avoid dwelling too much on the dark nights and poor
weather. It would suit many Cancerians to spend at least part of the
winter in warmer surroundings.

2 FRIDAY
Moon Age Day 15   Moon Sign Leo

am . . . .

pm . . . .
It's worth keeping a sense of proportion regarding any issue that seems difficult to resolve. Any difficulties that come your way at the moment are much more likely to be inspired by others and you may not be quite as inspirational in your approach to life as you were a few days ago. A little meditation might help.

3 SATURDAY
Moon Age Day 16   Moon Sign Leo

am . . . .

pm . . . .
If someone needs your help, you should be in exactly the right position to lend a hand. This is particularly true if they are going through something that you have experienced for yourself. Nobody is more empathic than those born under the zodiac sign of Cancer, and the more so when you are on familiar ground.

4 SUNDAY
Moon Age Day 17   Moon Sign Virgo

am . . . .

pm . . . .
You show strong enthusiasm for any challenge that comes along at the moment and you have what it takes to get through obstacles that might have proved too much for you in the past. Try not to achieve too much all at once, but use that natural patience of yours to get to your objectives sensibly and steadily.

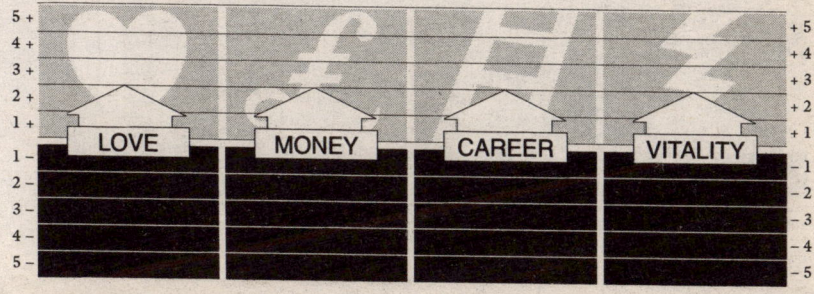

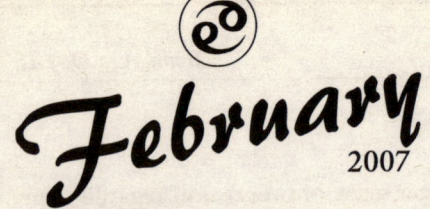

February
2007

YOUR MONTH AT A GLANCE

⊕ = Opportunities are around ⊖ = Be on the defensive ● = Life is pretty ordinary

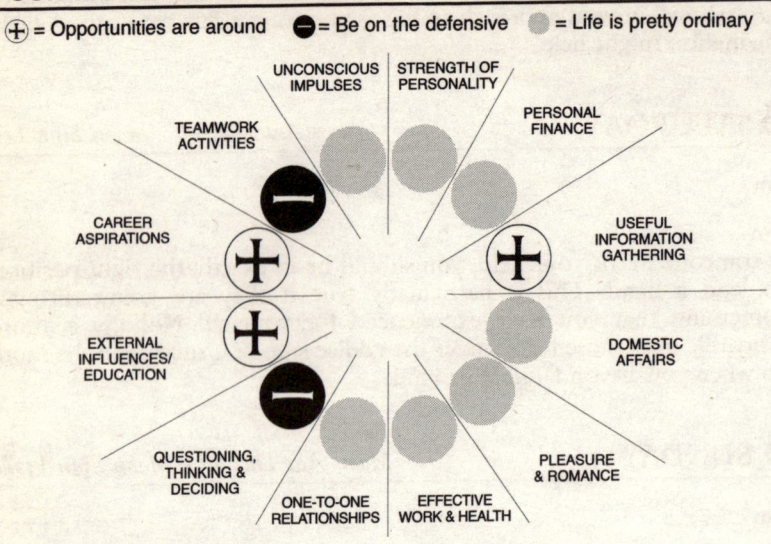

STRENGTH OF PERSONALITY

PERSONAL FINANCE

USEFUL INFORMATION GATHERING

DOMESTIC AFFAIRS

PLEASURE & ROMANCE

EFFECTIVE WORK & HEALTH

ONE-TO-ONE RELATIONSHIPS

QUESTIONING, THINKING & DECIDING

EXTERNAL INFLUENCES/ EDUCATION

CAREER ASPIRATIONS

TEAMWORK ACTIVITIES

UNCONSCIOUS IMPULSES

FEBRUARY HIGHS AND LOWS

Here I show you how the rhythms of the Moon will affect you this month. Like the tide, your energies and abilities will rise and fall with its pattern. When it is above the centre line, go for it, when it is below, you should be resting.

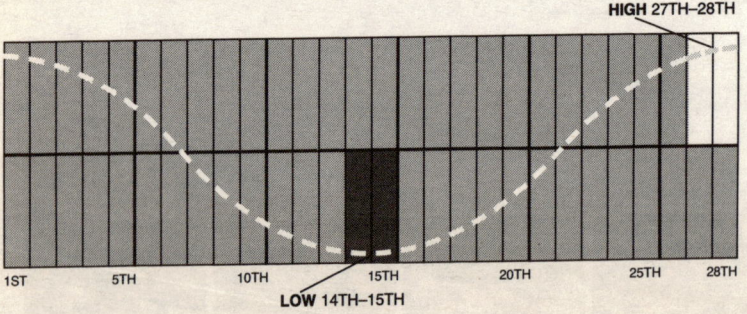

HIGH 27TH–28TH

1ST 5TH 10TH 15TH 20TH 25TH 28TH

LOW 14TH–15TH

52

5 MONDAY
Moon Age Day 18   Moon Sign Virgo

am . . . .

pm . . . .
It might be necessary to stand up for yourself in some way today. You are
not the sort of person to make a fuss unnecessarily, but when the chips
are down you simply won't be blamed for something you didn't do. In
fact, the sign of Cancer can be quite caustic when necessity arises.
Personal relationships should offer scope for enjoyment.

6 TUESDAY
Moon Age Day 19   Moon Sign Virgo

am . . . .

pm . . . .
The time is right to keep up your efforts to get cracking with new
projects. You can be very sure of yourself just now and this would be the
ideal period to push yourself a little. You can persuade colleagues and
friends to put a shoulder to the wheel if necessary, and you needn't go
short of compliments around this time.

7 WEDNESDAY
Moon Age Day 20   Moon Sign Libra

am . . . .

pm . . . .
Standard responses probably won't work at the moment. On the
contrary, you need to be original in your thinking and in the things you
are saying to others. It is possible to make significant progress in your life
at the moment, though you might have to pretend to be someone else if
a small amount of aggression is called for.

8 THURSDAY
Moon Age Day 21   Moon Sign Libra

am . . . .

pm . . . .
Planetary signs indicate that you might be being watched at the moment.
This isn't really surprising, particularly if you are putting on a fairly good
show. You have what it takes to keep the level of your popularity high,
and those Crabs who are presently between relationships could find new
love during this period.

9 FRIDAY
Moon Age Day 22   Moon Sign Scorpio

am . . . .

pm . . . .
A little confusion is possible when you are dealing with matters you don't understand very well. The best way forward is to ask someone who does know, as you could find their responses more than gratifying. All that is happening is that you are obtaining some of the many favours that others have had from you.

10 SATURDAY
Moon Age Day 23   Moon Sign Scorpio

am . . . .

pm . . . .
It is towards the social side of life that trends persuade you to turn your mind during this weekend. When it comes to business transactions of any sort or the offer of something that looks too good to be true, a bit of care is required. This is not the best time of the month during which to become involved in dubious projects.

11 SUNDAY
Moon Age Day 24   Moon Sign Scorpio

am . . . .

pm . . . .
This has potential to be a fairly relaxing day and one during which you have the necessary time to turn your attention towards home and family – always an important consideration as far as you are concerned. The week ahead requires some careful planning because there are good and bad aspects in the offing.

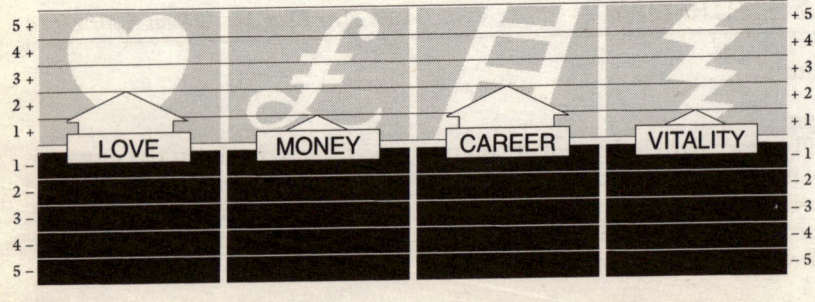

12 MONDAY   *Moon Age Day 25   Moon Sign Sagittarius*

am . . . .

pm . . . .
A day to keep abreast of news and things that are happening in your
home locality. It is possible that you might be called upon to act on
behalf of someone who is having a difficult time at the moment, and this
is one area in which you excel. You would be wise to avoid loud and
vexatious people if that proves to be possible.

13 TUESDAY   *Moon Age Day 26   Moon Sign Sagittarius*

am . . . .

pm . . . .
There are changes possible in your professional life. This may not be
quite as bad as it sounds, particularly if you can make sure you are made
responsible for something you find distinctly interesting.
Communication with someone you don't see too often is a possibility for
today.

14 WEDNESDAY   ☿   *Moon Age Day 27   Moon Sign Capricorn*

am . . . .

pm . . . .
There are a couple of days ahead during which exercising a little more
care would be no bad thing. The lunar low is inclined to bring you face
to face with situations you don't care for, and life can become distinctly
tedious in a number of ways. The best action is to ring the changes when
you can, but also to remain patient.

15 THURSDAY   ☿   *Moon Age Day 28   Moon Sign Capricorn*

am . . . .

pm . . . .
If your energy levels seem to be quite low at present, you could do worse
than to take some time to yourself. This isn't really a problem for you
because solitary moments can be quite appealing. Don't take on too
much and allow other people to do things for themselves, rather than
running round after them.

16 FRIDAY ☿ *Moon Age Day 0 Moon Sign Aquarius*

am . . . .

pm . . . .
A more active and enterprising day is possible for you and it is one during which you have to take the initiative if you want to get ahead. This should not be too difficult under present trends, and you might even decide you want to show a slightly more aggressive face to the world than would normally be the case.

17 SATURDAY ☿ *Moon Age Day 1 Moon Sign Aquarius*

am . . . .

pm . . . .
By all means keep in touch with people at a distance, but at the same time why not spend some time with family members during the weekend? Being amongst those you love is appealing to the Crab at any time, but right now there could be good family news, together with the realisation that someone is really growing up.

18 SUNDAY ☿ *Moon Age Day 2 Moon Sign Pisces*

am . . . .

pm . . . .
Standard responses sometimes won't work today, and you best option is to be original in your approach to others. Attitude is very important when you are approaching new hobbies or pastimes and these must represent something you find personally appealing. Trying to please others may not be enough now.

LOVE	MONEY	CAREER	VITALITY

19 MONDAY ☿ *Moon Age Day 3   Moon Sign Pisces*

am . . . .

pm . . . .
The start of a new week will offer you a chance to please others, and present planetary positions show you to be at your most charming. You may not respond very well to being told what to do, but you do have what it takes to break down barriers that could have existed in your life for quite some time.

20 TUESDAY ☿ *Moon Age Day 4   Moon Sign Aries*

am . . . .

pm . . . .
You can afford to refuse to be budged over any issue you see as being very important. Although you could be in for something of a struggle, those around you will gain a new respect for you when you stick up for yourself. Cancer can be very chatty at the moment and should respond positively to interesting and stimulating conversation.

21 WEDNESDAY ☿ *Moon Age Day 5   Moon Sign Aries*

am . . . .

pm . . . .
You would be wise to avoid confusion over issues that need to be resolved as early in the day as possible. If you have made up your mind to a particular course of action, it is important to stick to your guns. Not everyone will be happy with the situation, but you can't please all of the people all of the time.

22 THURSDAY ☿ *Moon Age Day 6   Moon Sign Taurus*

am . . . .

pm . . . .
Trends encourage you to broaden your horizons in some way. Cancer is now more progressive and forward-looking than has been the case since the start of the year. At the same time you have the potential to attract plenty of romantic responses and you might even have a new admirer.

23 FRIDAY ☿ *Moon Age Day 7   Moon Sign Taurus*

am . . . .

pm . . . .
The time is right to show tremendous enthusiasm for anything new and
exciting. So full is your social life likely to be around now that it might
be quite difficult to find the time necessary to get practical necessities out
of the way. Social arrangements might have to be altered, but in the main
this should be for the better.

24 SATURDAY ☿ *Moon Age Day 8   Moon Sign Gemini*

am . . . .

pm . . . .
The generally strong trends continue, though you might not be able to
achieve all you would wish with the arrival of the weekend. The answer
is simple – don't try! Instead of trying to get ahead in any way, why not
use today and tomorrow as periods in which you can enjoy yourself? You
can even persuade friends to join in.

25 SUNDAY ☿ *Moon Age Day 9   Moon Sign Gemini*

am . . . .

pm . . . .
There is likely to be a strong sense of that Cancerian conscience pushing
you along today, and much of what you do is undertaken simply because
you feel it is the 'right' thing to do. Sometimes your judgement on this
is sound, but there are times when you don't owe anything and should
be feathering your own nest instead.

	LOVE	MONEY	CAREER	VITALITY
5 +				+ 5
4 +				+ 4
3 +				+ 3
2 +				+ 2
1 +				+ 1
1 −				− 1
2 −				− 2
3 −				− 3
4 −				− 4
5 −				− 5

26 MONDAY ☿ *Moon Age Day 10 Moon Sign Gemini*

am . . . .

pm . . . .
Even if the start of a new working week seems slightly quieter than of
late, this is a very temporary interlude because by tomorrow you can get
yourself on the boil again. For the moment, it's worth clearing the decks
for action and preparing yourself for what might be the most hectic
interlude that February has to offer.

27 TUESDAY ☿ *Moon Age Day 11 Moon Sign Cancer*

am . . . .

pm . . . .
There is good company about as the lunar high comes along, and this can
make all the difference to your own attitude and actions. If you get Lady
Luck definitely on your side you can afford to take a few chances, and can
make sure that no one misses out on the absolutely charming and yet
very dynamic Crab that is on offer.

28 WEDNESDAY ☿ *Moon Age Day 12 Moon Sign Cancer*

am . . . .

pm . . . .
Confidence remains high and you might even decide to tackle things you
have shied away from in the past. Don't hold back, especially when you
know something that could be to your own advantage and that of the
people you care for. Almost any course of action is legitimate with the
Moon in your own zodiac sign.

1 THURSDAY ☿ *Moon Age Day 13 Moon Sign Leo*

am . . . .

pm . . . .
It's the beginning of a new month, and although the Moon has now
moved on, it looks as though you have as much scope as ever to make
progress. Not everyone has your best interests at heart and you need to
be careful who you trust for the next day or two. Simply rely on that
powerful intuition.

2 FRIDAY ☿ *Moon Age Day 14   Moon Sign Leo*

am . . . .

pm . . . .
You may already have got yourself into a weekend frame of mind, in which case some of the trials and tribulations of your working life might not appeal very much. Nevertheless you tend to soldier on because that is the way you are made. By the evening you might decide to spread your wings socially.

3 SATURDAY ☿ *Moon Age Day 15   Moon Sign Virgo*

am . . . .

pm . . . .
You are born of the most caring and considerate of all the zodiac signs and you know instinctively when to offer the sort of advice and practical support that is most needed. Even if not everyone you set out to help seems that grateful, it is how you feel inside that matters the most.

4 SUNDAY ☿ *Moon Age Day 16   Moon Sign Virgo*

am . . . .

pm . . . .
Trends suggest you might feel slightly uncomfortable if you know that others are putting you on some sort of pedestal. This uneasy feeling is understandable but not logical. Have confidence in yourself because you shouldn't let anyone down and can come up with the goods whenever it proves necessary today.

	LOVE	MONEY	CAREER	VITALITY
5 +				+ 5
4 +				+ 4
3 +				+ 3
2 +				+ 2
1 +				+ 1
1 -				- 1
2 -				- 2
3 -				- 3
4 -				- 4
5 -				- 5

March 2007

YOUR MONTH AT A GLANCE

⊕ = Opportunities are around   ⊖ = Be on the defensive   ⬤ = Life is pretty ordinary

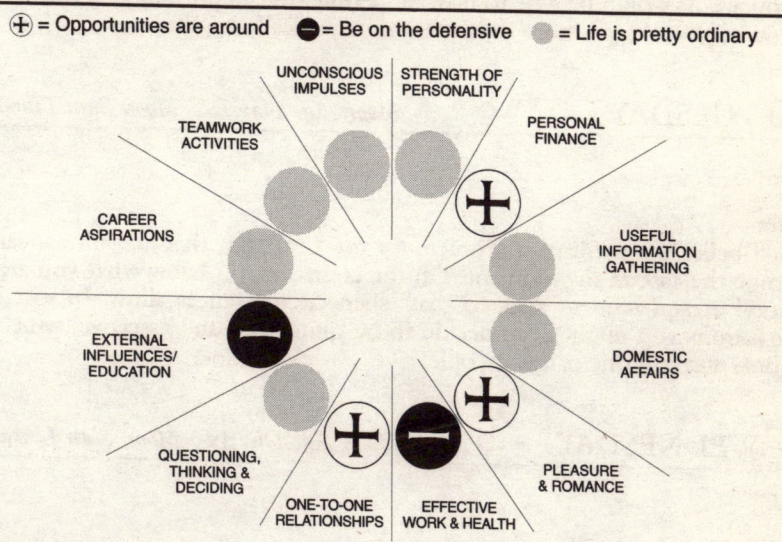

MARCH HIGHS AND LOWS

Here I show you how the rhythms of the Moon will affect you this month. Like the tide, your energies and abilities will rise and fall with its pattern. When it is above the centre line, go for it, when it is below, you should be resting.

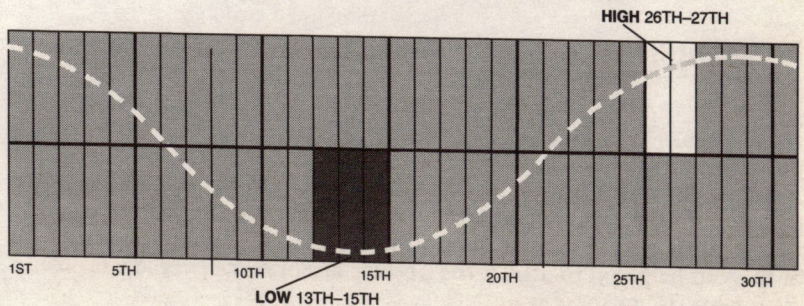

5 MONDAY ☿ *Moon Age Day 17   Moon Sign Virgo*

am . . . .

pm . . . .
The focus is on doing your best to please others at the moment, and you should have little difficulty proving just how conscientious and caring you are. It would be wise to take some time over important jobs because you might take on more than you can realistically handle.

6 TUESDAY ☿ *Moon Age Day 18   Moon Sign Libra*

am . . . .

pm . . . .
Self-belief is sometimes a problem for the Crab, but that doesn't appear to be the case at the moment. On the contrary, you know what you are good at and tend to stick to that when circumstances allow. In social situations you might even decide to be quite bold and assertive, which could surprise one or two people.

7 WEDNESDAY ☿ *Moon Age Day 19   Moon Sign Libra*

am . . . .

pm . . . .
You can use your positive outlook to make you quite popular today, and you might be especially successful when with groups of people. Your social conscience could easily be aroused by events that happen in your locality, and as is usually the case for the Crab, you might be doing what you can to help others.

8 THURSDAY ☿ *Moon Age Day 20   Moon Sign Scorpio*

am . . . .

pm . . . .
A day to put your business and financial acumen to the test and to prove to yourself how capable you are. It appears that you can get ahead quite well in those situations that demand that extra bit of common sense. All of this can help you to attract the positive attention of people who could assist your rise in some way.

9 FRIDAY

Moon Age Day 21   Moon Sign Scorpio

am . . . .

pm . . . .
Even if you tend to be somewhat more thoughtful today, this is no bad thing. Present trends encourage you to mull things over more, but the conclusions you reach are far from being theoretical and have genuine practical value. Standing up for the rights of others will not be far from your mind at any time this month.

10 SATURDAY

Moon Age Day 22   Moon Sign Scorpio

am . . . .

pm . . . .
You can use your natural warmth to bring joy to others and it seems you simply cannot help being liked. This should ensure you of a great deal of positive attention during the weekend and you might have to run to catch up with all the possibilities that are on offer. It's worth breaking a particular problem down into its component parts in order to solve it.

11 SUNDAY

Moon Age Day 23   Moon Sign Sagittarius

am . . . .

pm . . . .
You seem to be in the mood for planning – maybe for a journey that comes a little further down the line. Co-operation with family members is apt to be good and there could be a lot of happiness about at the moment. Try for something different today, particularly if you don't feel like committing yourself to too many routines.

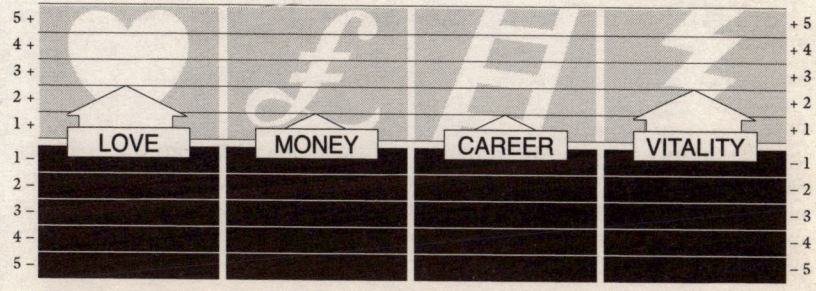

12 MONDAY *Moon Age Day 24   Moon Sign Sagittarius*

am . . . .

pm . . . .
You would be wise to put in that extra bit of effort today that could make all the difference in the longer term. It might not always be easy to bring others round to your way of thinking, but a little persistence can work wonders. You have no reason to doubt either your popularity or your ability to use it to your advantage.

13 TUESDAY *Moon Age Day 25   Moon Sign Capricorn*

am . . . .

pm . . . .
Things could slow somewhat as the lunar low comes around again. This day would be better for planning than doing, and you could find those around you slightly more difficult to deal with than has been the case recently. Try to maintain an optimistic attitude just now, even when things go wrong.

14 WEDNESDAY *Moon Age Day 26   Moon Sign Capricorn*

am . . . .

pm . . . .
This is no time to be pushing your luck. Gambling is not your best option at present, and you do best when you stick to tasks you both like and understand. Be prepared to follow the lead of others, and when you have the chance, to use their knowledge and common sense in order to leapfrog any potentially difficult situations.

15 THURSDAY *Moon Age Day 27   Moon Sign Capricorn*

am . . . .

pm . . . .
Trends suggest that life will remain essentially quiet through the first part of today, though you should be able to change things in the afternoon. Slowly but surely you can get on top of any issues that might have been worrying you, and the more optimistic attitude that has been predominating so far this month soon returns.

16 FRIDAY   *Moon Age Day 28   Moon Sign Aquarius*

am . . . .

pm . . . .
Intimate family relationships are well accented today, together with romantic attachments that also look particularly good. In a conversational sense you may not be dealing with matters of earth-shattering importance, but even small talk has its place in your life right now.

17 SATURDAY   *Moon Age Day 29   Moon Sign Aquarius*

am . . . .

pm . . . .
You are in a position to enjoy harmony and co-operation and to show your real Cancerian traits at present. What you are looking for is the sort of happiness that makes you glad to be alive and this is not especially difficult to find. Your inner confidence has the power to help you overcome any jitters.

18 SUNDAY   *Moon Age Day 0   Moon Sign Pisces*

am . . . .

pm . . . .
You need to push ahead as much as possible right now, even if this proves to be rather difficult on a Sunday. Now is the time to plan for what you want to achieve in a practical sense in the days ahead and to enlist the help and support of family members. Cancer is very tidy-minded under present trends so you will probably hate clutter.

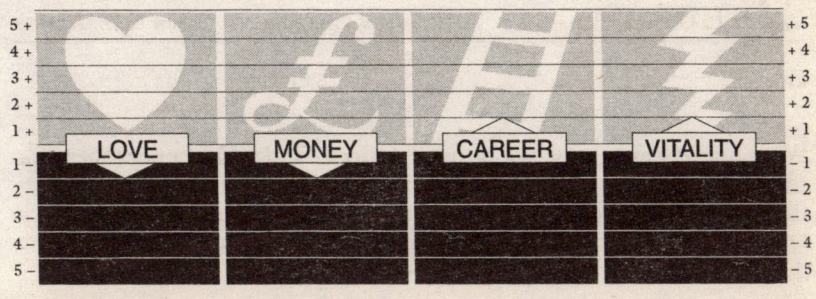

19 MONDAY
Moon Age Day 1   Moon Sign Pisces

am . . . .

pm . . . .
Harmony and co-operation remain the keywords for you and that is fairly normal for your zodiac sign. What you don't care for are arguments of any sort, and you would probably run ten miles today to avoid one. Nevertheless, it's worth making it plain that you won't be messed about or misused.

20 TUESDAY
Moon Age Day 2   Moon Sign Aries

am . . . .

pm . . . .
This may be one of the best days of the month for pleasant relationships and for turning social advantages into business opportunities. Trends suggest that just about everyone you meet today seems to have something good to say to and about you. You can use such compliments to boost your ego and that can only be a positive thing.

21 WEDNESDAY
Moon Age Day 3   Moon Sign Aries

am . . . .

pm . . . .
With more in the way of responsibility coming in all the time, this is one of those days during which you might have to break into a run in order to get everything done. That shouldn't really matter if you make use of all your energy and your ability to know instinctively how to respond to almost any situation.

22 THURSDAY
Moon Age Day 4   Moon Sign Taurus

am . . . .

pm . . . .
What matters most now is a positive outlook, and with support there for the taking from a number of different astrological directions it seems as though you have what it takes to make significant ground in your life generally. Romance has potential to blossom too, even if you have to give it a little nudge.

23 FRIDAY

Moon Age Day 5   Moon Sign Taurus

am . . . .

pm . . . .
Any sporting activity suits you under present trends and you could well
be quite anxious to be a winner. This could go against the grain as far as
part of your mind is concerned, because if you win, that means someone
else must lose. Don't be afraid to put such thoughts out of your head and
simply respond to the challenge.

24 SATURDAY

Moon Age Day 6   Moon Sign Gemini

am . . . .

pm . . . .
After a few potentially very hectic days you can slow things down
somewhat for the weekend. The Moon is now in your solar twelfth house
and that encourages a more contemplative frame of mind. This would be
an ideal time to spend extra hours with close family members and
especially with your partner.

25 SUNDAY

Moon Age Day 7   Moon Sign Gemini

am . . . .

pm . . . .
Your ambitions could well be hampered at the moment, and in order to
circumnavigate the worst effects of that twelfth-house Moon you need to
deal with matters that are of no real consequence. Slow and steady wins
the race, though in all honesty this is not the time either to be
competitive or to take risks.

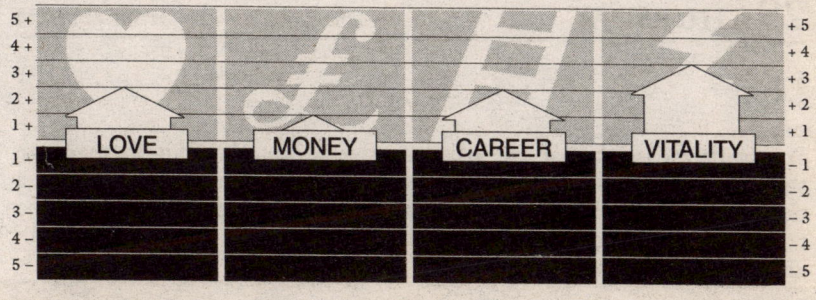

26 MONDAY
Moon Age Day 8   Moon Sign Cancer

am . . . .

pm . . . .
All of a sudden you can make your mind work very differently and there could hardly be a better planetary line-up for starting a new working week than the one that surrounds you now. The lunar high gives you all the incentive you could possibly need to get ahead, and every advantage now looks as big as a bus from your perspective.

27 TUESDAY
Moon Age Day 9   Moon Sign Cancer

am . . . .

pm . . . .
You now need to be pushing ahead with all guns blazing. What you do today can have a great bearing on both the short- and long-term future, and if you remain competent, forward-looking and even somewhat aggressive, the world won't stand in your way. Refuse to be beaten because you can break your own records right now.

28 WEDNESDAY
Moon Age Day 10   Moon Sign Leo

am . . . .

pm . . . .
Today is good for practical developments, even if there are few irritating delays to be dealt with. If you have gained great pace during the last couple of days, you probably won't take kindly to being stopped in your tracks. You have what it takes to persuade others to move aside for the steamroller you have become.

29 THURSDAY
Moon Age Day 11   Moon Sign Leo

am . . . .

pm . . . .
It is romantic issues that can make you feel good today. Whether you are sixteen or sixty, single or married, already settled or in the market for a new love, today is for you. It appears that you can help yourself best by telling your lover exactly how you feel. Emotions run deep for the Crab, and others should know it!

30 FRIDAY
Moon Age Day 12   Moon Sign Leo

am . . . .

pm . . . .
Information is on offer from every conceivable direction at the moment, and simply keeping up with the pace of life can be difficult enough. It would be best to stick to an ordered routine if you want to get everything done, but it is unlikely that life itself will offer you that opportunity. As a result, thinking on your feet counts for a great deal.

31 SATURDAY
Moon Age Day 13   Moon Sign Virgo

am . . . .

pm . . . .
Problems must be attacked, because the more issues you put on the shelf today, the greater will be your need to deal with all of them at once tomorrow. You have what it takes to be definite, decisive and assertive. There are certain situations in which others won't like this Crab, but that's just too bad for them.

1 SUNDAY
Moon Age Day 14   Moon Sign Virgo

am . . . .

pm . . . .
The start of a new month continues the generally favourable trends that predominated during March. You needn't be any sort of April Fool today, and can show the world just how capable and dynamic you are capable of being. Others may slow down to accommodate the fact that this is a Sunday, but you may decide that isn't necessary.

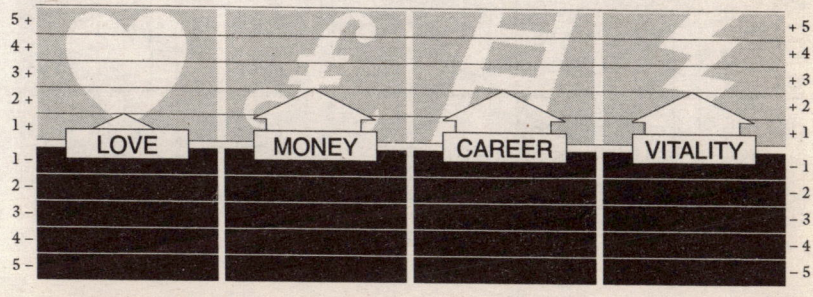

April 2007

YOUR MONTH AT A GLANCE

⊕ = Opportunities are around   ⊖ = Be on the defensive   ⬤ = Life is pretty ordinary

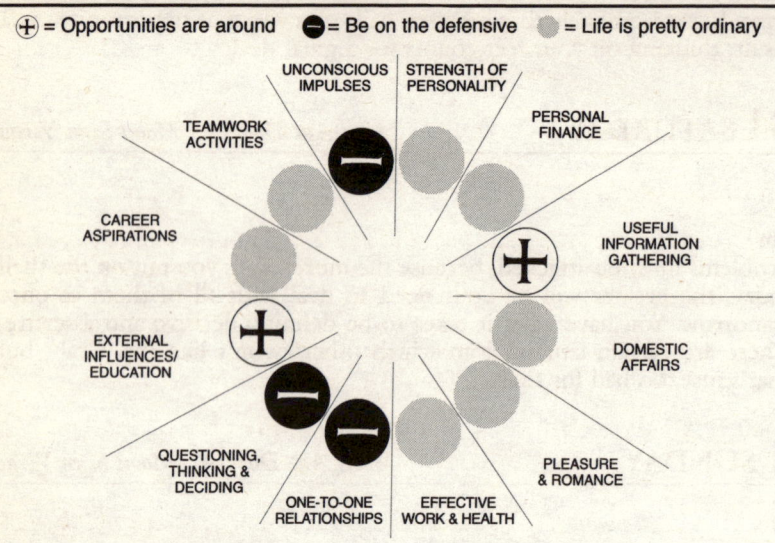

APRIL HIGHS AND LOWS

Here I show you how the rhythms of the Moon will affect you this month. Like the tide, your energies and abilities will rise and fall with its pattern. When it is above the centre line, go for it, when it is below, you should be resting.

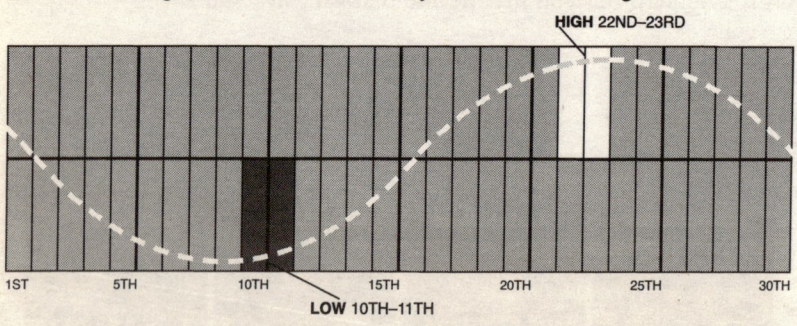

HIGH 22ND–23RD

LOW 10TH–11TH

70

2 MONDAY

Moon Age Day 15 Moon Sign Libra

am ....

pm ....
It is communication issues that make life look especially interesting at present. You may not always understand what those around you are talking about, but you do have what it takes to bluff your way through certain situations. Once you have time to reflect, everything should become clearer.

3 TUESDAY

Moon Age Day 16 Moon Sign Libra

am ....

pm ....
Romance should be making you feel good, and if it is not, perhaps you are doing something slightly wrong. You can attract attention from not one but several directions, and even if this is nothing more than flirting, it can help you to raise your self-esteem somewhat.

4 WEDNESDAY

Moon Age Day 17 Moon Sign Libra

am ....

pm ....
There could be a little more in the way of pessimism about today, particularly if you are expected to do something that takes more confidence than you think you possess. It's time to take your courage in both your hands and to push forward. That's your best chance to make sure everything turns out right in the end.

5 THURSDAY

Moon Age Day 18 Moon Sign Scorpio

am ....

pm ....
Stumbling blocks are a possibility at the moment, especially on those occasions when you are not directly in command of your own destiny. This is not the best of times for trusting people you doubt and wherever possible you should take the lead. Group activities in particular are best with you at the helm.

6 FRIDAY
Moon Age Day 19   Moon Sign Scorpio

am . . . .

pm . . . .
Beware of a little sentimentality creeping in today because it could take the edge off your natural abilities and prevent you from making the sort of progress you most need right now. The Cancerian mind is apt to look to the past, but there is little help there for you at this time.

7 SATURDAY
Moon Age Day 20   Moon Sign Sagittarius

am . . . .

pm . . . .
There could be a few hiccups to deal with, but these needn't hold you back too much. You can even persuade strangers to support you, and to prove conclusively that they have your best interests at heart. You might enjoy a shopping spree this weekend, particularly if there are some bargains around.

8 SUNDAY
Moon Age Day 21   Moon Sign Sagittarius

am . . . .

pm . . . .
Rather than simply looking at problems, why not attack them as early in the day as you can? That will leave you the time you need to do what pleases you. The Crab needs luxury in its life, even if this is sometimes sacrificed to the needs of others. A day to treat yourself a little and allow those around you to spoil you because you deserve it!

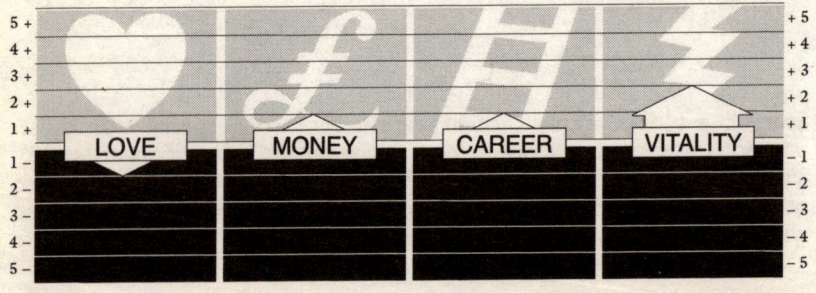

9 MONDAY   *Moon Age Day 22   Moon Sign Sagittarius*

am . . . .

pm . . . .
Any improvements that are possible today are likely to be thanks to loved ones and special friends. You could be feeling rather nostalgic at the moment and maybe looking back at special moments you would love to relive. That isn't possible, but you can make sure there are new red-letter days soon.

10 TUESDAY   *Moon Age Day 23   Moon Sign Capricorn*

am . . . .

pm . . . .
The lunar low is unlikely to have too much of an impact on your life this month because there are so many planetary influences that support you at the moment. All the same it would be better to avoid taking chances today and gambling is certainly out. It's worth listening to what a friend is trying to tell you.

11 WEDNESDAY   *Moon Age Day 24   Moon Sign Capricorn*

am . . . .

pm . . . .
You want to look forward, especially in a professional sense, but there are a great many variables to bear in mind. It might be better to let things ride for a day or two, whilst you concentrate on making yourself more comfortable in a general sense. Once again you can take advantage of the kindness of those around you.

12 THURSDAY   *Moon Age Day 25   Moon Sign Aquarius*

am . . . .

pm . . . .
When it comes to negotiations of any sort it seems that you can be very persuasive at present, and there are few people around who could refuse you any reasonable request. You should remain basically flexible, and therein lies part of the secret of your present success. If you can make sure that people like you, that is half the battle won.

13 FRIDAY

Moon Age Day 26   Moon Sign Aquarius

am . . . .

pm . . . .
You may feel that home is the best place to be right now, particularly if something in the outside world feels slightly threatening. What a great time this would be for a reunion of some sort, or for getting in touch with people who for one reason or another you haven't seen recently.

14 SATURDAY

Moon Age Day 27   Moon Sign Pisces

am . . . .

pm . . . .
This would be one of the best times of the month for starting a new project, though this is likely to be something that is associated with leisure or pleasure, rather than a work-related matter. New groups or associations can come into your life around now and they tend to offer a different way of thinking for the Crab.

15 SUNDAY

Moon Age Day 28   Moon Sign Pisces

am . . . .

pm . . . .
If progress is a little slack, you can at least tell yourself that this, after all, a Sunday and is meant to be a day of rest. You can afford to take time out to be with your partner or family members and to find new ways to relax. If you are a Crab who is soon going on a journey, this might be a good time to arrange those last-minute details.

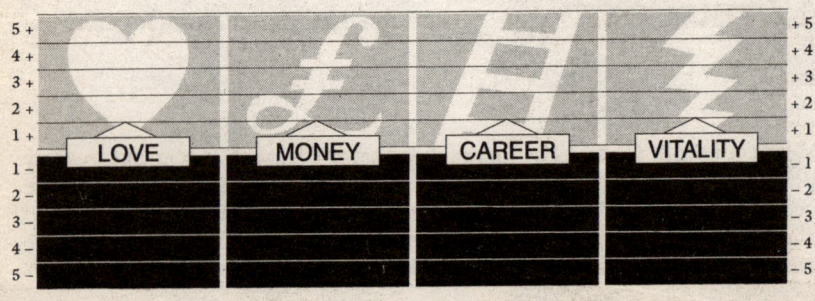

16 MONDAY
Moon Age Day 29   Moon Sign Aries

am . . . .

pm . . . .
At the start of a new working week you should have plenty of energy available to pour into your work. Cancer is extremely capable at this time, and the support of the planet Mars in particular encourages you to be more decisive, but possibly also slightly more touchy than would normally be the case.

17 TUESDAY
Moon Age Day 0   Moon Sign Aries

am . . . .

pm . . . .
You may not feel especially settled right now, and it is true that a restless phase is indicated in your solar chart. It might be hard to work out exactly why you are slightly ill at ease and there may be little you can do to remedy this situation. Bear in mind that time itself could well sort matters out in a day or two.

18 WEDNESDAY
Moon Age Day 1   Moon Sign Taurus

am . . . .

pm . . . .
There could be some very favourable times on offer in terms of your romantic life and you should ensure you are in the right frame of mind to respond positively to these. If your popularity is high at present, it is also possible for you to attract compliments from some fairly unexpected directions. Try to take these in your stride.

19 THURSDAY
Moon Age Day 2   Moon Sign Taurus

am . . . .

pm . . . .
Cancer could now be showing especially good leadership qualities, and although it isn't too common for the Crab to take the initiative in group situations, that is exactly what you have scope to do now. Your confidence and self-assured attitude might surprise a few people, but it can certainly prove to be useful.

20 FRIDAY

Moon Age Day 3   Moon Sign Gemini

am . . . .

pm . . . .

There are opposing trends around for today and tomorrow. Part of your mind could be telling you to push ahead and to make those all-important decisions, whilst the fact that the Moon is in your solar twelfth house might be holding you back. If you are really unsure, you may decide to wait until after the weekend.

21 SATURDAY

Moon Age Day 4   Moon Sign Gemini

am . . . .

pm . . . .

You have what it takes to make something very special of this weekend. As far as today is concerned, trends encourage a quiet but attentive approach, and just the right frame of mind to get something positive from an outing. You should find ways to feed your intellect, and anything historical could really appeal now.

22 SUNDAY

Moon Age Day 5   Moon Sign Cancer

am . . . .

pm . . . .

The Moon races into the sign of Cancer, where it is happier than in any other section of the zodiac. That is fortunate indeed for you, and the lunar high assists you to be at your most positive and go-getting. Even if you are still be in the mood for getting away from routines, you might also be more adventurous.

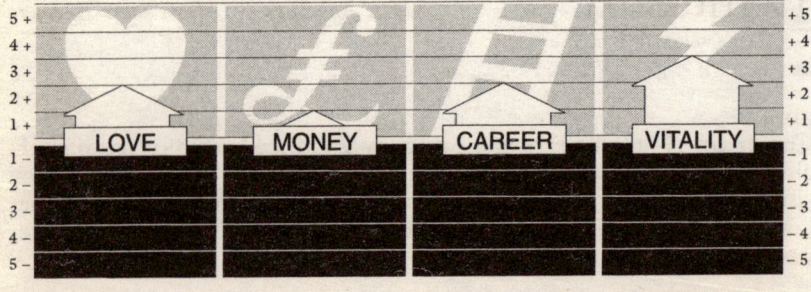

23 MONDAY   *Moon Age Day 6   Moon Sign Cancer*

am . . . .

pm . . . .
You can make this a very positive start to a new week, and if you are in a position of some authority at work, this is a period during which you could well attract the attention of superiors. As a rule this might make you very nervous, but the lunar high allows you to take almost anything in your stride.

24 TUESDAY   *Moon Age Day 7   Moon Sign Leo*

am . . . .

pm . . . .
It is towards short-term goals that your mind is apt to turn right now, at least partly because you want to see things getting done. New starts are quite possible and you may not have quite as much patience as would usually be the case, especially with individuals who jump about from one foot to the other.

25 WEDNESDAY   *Moon Age Day 8   Moon Sign Leo*

am . . . .

pm . . . .
When you have spoken your mind it would sensible to stick to your guns. You can gain the respect of others if you refuse to back down, and in the end can persuade them to come round to your point of view in any case. Cancer may not often appear to be the strongest zodiac sign in the bunch, but it seems to be so now.

26 THURSDAY   *Moon Age Day 9   Moon Sign Leo*

am . . . .

pm . . . .
A developing tendency towards daydreaming could well become obvious as today advances. There is nothing at all wrong with this, just as long as you keep at least one foot in the real world. Once the cares of the day are out of the way, you might decide to disappear into the pages of a really good book.

27 FRIDAY

Moon Age Day 10   Moon Sign Virgo

am . . . .

pm . . . .
If you are too impulsive today, the result can be misunderstandings. It is still good to do things your own way but the odd explanation would help. With the weekend in view you need to be planning something that takes you completely out of yourself. Contact with friends is well starred around this time.

28 SATURDAY

Moon Age Day 11   Moon Sign Virgo

am . . . .

pm . . . .
In some ways it could seem as though you are miles from getting exactly what you want the most, but if you look at matters objectively you should see that progress is being made. A day to get away from the routine cares of life and do something that makes you feel good to be alive.

29 SUNDAY

Moon Age Day 12   Moon Sign Libra

am . . . .

pm . . . .
You have scope to mix with interesting characters today, and you should find a good deal of enjoyment from simply being in their company. Yours tends to be more of a supportive role than has been the case in recent days and you may well be happy enough to stand just one step out of the limelight for the moment.

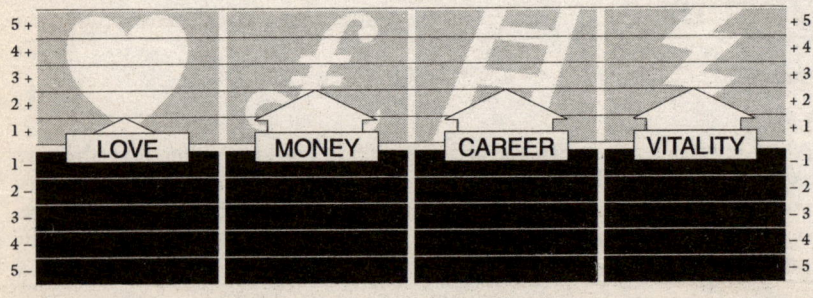

30 MONDAY
Moon Age Day 13   Moon Sign Libra

am . . . .

pm . . . .
Your powers of attraction are now strong and this applies every bit as
much in your practical life as it does at a personal level. If there is
something you really want but about which you have been afraid to ask,
now is the time to take your courage in both your hands. Few reasonable
requests should be denied you at present.

1 TUESDAY
Moon Age Day 14   Moon Sign Libra

am . . . .

pm . . . .
The deep need for security that so typifies your zodiac sign is clearly on
display at the moment. This is unlikely to be a go-getting sort of day and
represents a period during which you are consciously watching and
waiting. There are situations in which you might have to force yourself
to be more decisive.

2 WEDNESDAY
Moon Age Day 15   Moon Sign Scorpio

am . . . .

pm . . . .
Romance receives a boost from the planet of love and you can pep up
your love life no end around now. New and positive influences are
coming along, and as the day unfolds you could discover that you are
feeling more and more confident. It's worth giving some thought to
travel plans, particularly if a journey is just around the corner.

3 THURSDAY
Moon Age Day 16   Moon Sign Scorpio

am . . . .

pm . . . .
Input and information is especially important and you need to keep your
eyes and ears wide open to what is going on around you. The most casual
of conversations can carry important messages and you need to be awake
to the possibilities that are available from a host of different and
sometimes surprising directions.

4 FRIDAY
Moon Age Day 17   Moon Sign Sagittarius

am . . . .

pm . . . .
It's posssible that some of your most carefully laid schemes could go slightly wrong today, and much of your time is likely to be spent 'tweaking'. When you do have moments to yourself you may well be thinking about either luxury or security – two of the most important factors to the average Crab.

5 SATURDAY
Moon Age Day 18   Moon Sign Sagittarius

am . . . .

pm . . . .
Trends encourage you to turn your mind towards domestic matters and to changes you want to make around you that will make life more comfortable in the longer term. New projects may well be put on hold, maybe until well into the start of the new week. If chaos rules for friends, perhaps they need your assistance.

6 SUNDAY
Moon Age Day 19   Moon Sign Sagittarius

am . . . .

pm . . . .
A day to relax and watch, because for the moment planetary influences are not right for positive action on any front. You can't lose anything by taking a rest, and once you have done so you see things much clearer. Prepare yourself for the start of a new working week that will have its share of challenges.

	LOVE	MONEY	CAREER	VITALITY
5 +					+ 5
4 +					+ 4
3 +					+ 3
2 +					+ 2
1 +					+ 1
1 –					– 1
2 –					– 2
3 –					– 3
4 –					– 4
5 –					– 5

May 2007

Your Month At A Glance

⊕ = Opportunities are around   ⊜ = Be on the defensive   ⬤ = Life is pretty ordinary

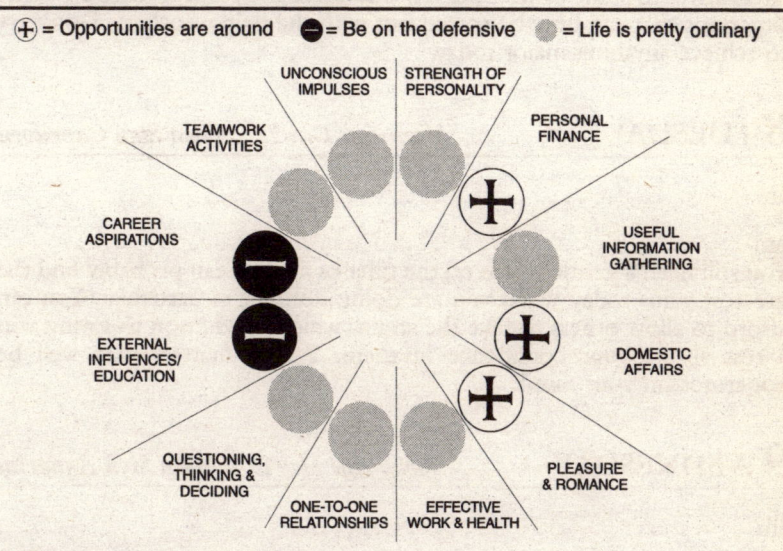

TEAMWORK ACTIVITIES

UNCONSCIOUS IMPULSES

STRENGTH OF PERSONALITY

PERSONAL FINANCE

CAREER ASPIRATIONS

USEFUL INFORMATION GATHERING

EXTERNAL INFLUENCES/ EDUCATION

DOMESTIC AFFAIRS

QUESTIONING, THINKING & DECIDING

ONE-TO-ONE RELATIONSHIPS

EFFECTIVE WORK & HEALTH

PLEASURE & ROMANCE

May Highs and Lows

Here I show you how the rhythms of the Moon will affect you this month. Like the tide, your energies and abilities will rise and fall with its pattern. When it is above the centre line, go for it, when it is below, you should be resting.

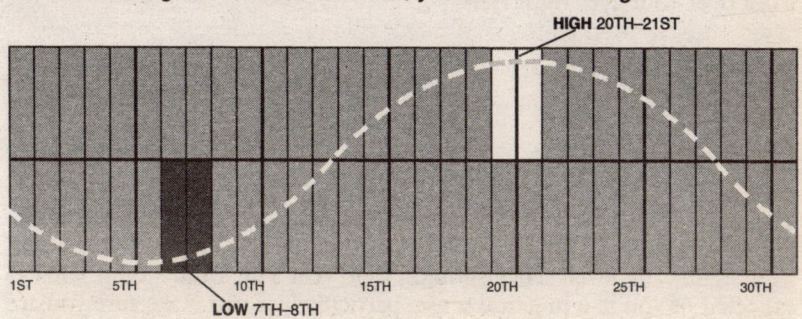

HIGH 20TH–21ST

1ST   5TH   10TH   15TH   20TH   25TH   30TH

LOW 7TH–8TH

7 MONDAY   *Moon Age Day 20   Moon Sign Capricorn*

am . . . .

pm . . . .
Be prepared to take practical advice today because chances are you will
need it. The lunar low is around and although you might be able to find
alternatives to some of your plans if they go slightly amiss, there are other
situations that can only be sorted out with the help of others. Don't try
to achieve anything major today.

8 TUESDAY   *Moon Age Day 21   Moon Sign Capricorn*

am . . . .

pm . . . .
You still need a gentle touch on the tiller of life and can probably find the
greatest gains today when you are doing nothing in particular. You can
afford to allow others to take the strain, which in addition to giving you
a rest shows your confidence in them. Family matters may well be
uppermost in your mind.

9 WEDNESDAY   *Moon Age Day 22   Moon Sign Aquarius*

am . . . .

pm . . . .
Things should be generally back to normal as the Moon moves into
Aquarius. However, 'normal' is a relative term because there are other
planets around at present that enhance your intuition to the point at
which others may call you a little spooky. You needn't let anyone pull the
wool over your eyes right now.

10 THURSDAY   *Moon Age Day 23   Moon Sign Aquarius*

am . . . .

pm . . . .
There could be a new love interest on the horizon for some Crabs at the
moment, and for many of you it will be relationships that fill your mind
to a significant level. That shouldn't prevent you from doing what is
expected of you in a practical sense, particularly if you make sure you are
efficient and cheerful in your work.

11 FRIDAY
Moon Age Day 24   Moon Sign Pisces

am . . . .

pm . . . .
Any increase in the pressure you feel being placed upon you can be accommodated easily, even if you panic at first. It's worth getting yourself sorted out before you tackle anything new, and this is especially important if you find that you will have to address a number of people. Public speaking isn't usually your thing.

12 SATURDAY
Moon Age Day 25   Moon Sign Pisces

am . . . .

pm . . . .
There is no doubt that the level of your curiosity is turned up full today. There isn't a stone on the path of life that you can't turn over, just to see what is beneath it. Some might call you nosey, but if you don't carry out your own enquiries, how are you to know the right way forward when it matters the most?

13 SUNDAY
Moon Age Day 26   Moon Sign Pisces

am . . . .

pm . . . .
It would be best to avoid arguments today, though this might be easier said than done as far as family members are concerned. It's possible that there is someone close to you who has to question everything you say and do. If you can avoid rising to the bait, so much the better, because there is little to gain from responding.

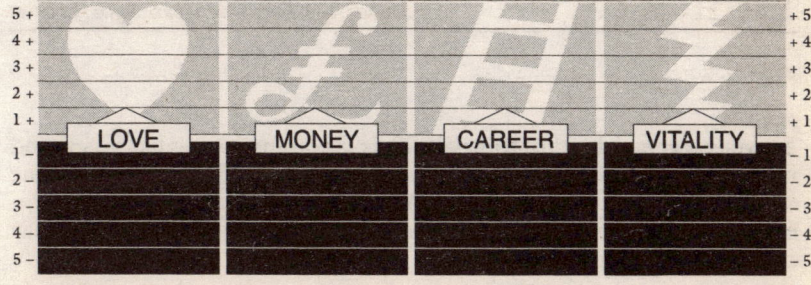

14 MONDAY   *Moon Age Day 27   Moon Sign Aries*

am . . . .

pm . . . .
You can benefit today from any sort of extrovert activity and from being
involved in physical work of some sort. As far as your intellect is
concerned, there is little or nothing that goes over your head. Ordinary
rules and regulations may prove to be somewhat annoying, especially if
they stop you in your tracks.

15 TUESDAY   *Moon Age Day 28   Moon Sign Aries*

am . . . .

pm . . . .
There are gains available if you make yourself generally useful today and
be where things are happening. You won't help your cause by sitting in
a corner on your own and simply getting on with things. Present trends
show that the more you advertise your presence, the greater is the chance
that you can get your point of view taken on board.

16 WEDNESDAY   *Moon Age Day 29   Moon Sign Taurus*

am . . . .

pm . . . .
It is within social situations that you can get your winning ways to shine
out at the moment. Although you can make progress of a practical sort,
the best enjoyment and the greatest advances are possible when you are
mixing with people who interest you. Cancer can be easily bored by
routines around now.

17 THURSDAY   *Moon Age Day 0   Moon Sign Taurus*

am . . . .

pm . . . .
Trends suggest that your domestic life is becoming as good as it gets and
at least part of this is down to your own attitude. If there has been some
sort of discord, you are the one who has what it takes to put things right.
Even if you have had no direct involvement in such situations you may
well end up being the peacemaker.

18 FRIDAY   *Moon Age Day 1   Moon Sign Gemini*

am . . . .

pm . . . .
Relationships should continue to be quite rewarding, but with the Moon
now moving into your solar twelfth house you could be entering a more
contemplative phase. This happens to the Crab now and again, and the
people who know you the best are well aware of the fact. This is a good
time to solve puzzles.

19 SATURDAY   *Moon Age Day 2   Moon Sign Gemini*

am . . . .

pm . . . .
There are new interests on the horizon, some of which allow you to go
to places both inside and outside your head where you haven't been
before. You can now display the more unusual of your qualities, and
make yourself curious and fascinating to others. Cancerian people can be
deep and unfathomable pools!

20 SUNDAY   *Moon Age Day 3   Moon Sign Cancer*

am . . . .

pm . . . .
Any tendency towards introspection is now clearly out of the window in
a flash. The lunar high arrives and enables you to get firmly in the driving
seat. Don't be tardy about making up your mind in any situation, and let
the world know that you are ready to take command. New and better
responsibilities could be the result.

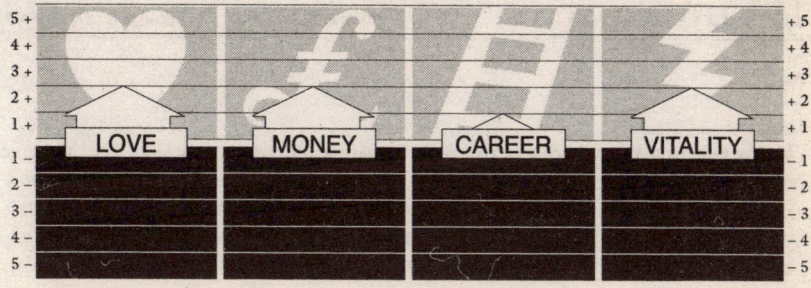

21 MONDAY
Moon Age Day 4   Moon Sign Cancer

am . . . .

pm . . . .
If you were slightly thwarted in your intentions yesterday because it was
a Sunday, the same cannot be said to be the case today. The time is right
to push ahead with your plans and not to take no for an answer. You
should be able to strengthen your finances and make use of a strong
element of good luck.

22 TUESDAY
Moon Age Day 5   Moon Sign Leo

am . . . .

pm . . . .
Once again that insatiable curiosity wins out, as it will at any time during
this month that things quieten down a little. You want to know how
everything works and there is great intellectual stimulation at every turn.
A break from routine would probably be good, even though you might
have to leave something until later as a result.

23 WEDNESDAY
Moon Age Day 6   Moon Sign Leo

am . . . .

pm . . . .
You need plenty of variety and stimulation if you are to function at your
best right now. The Crab becomes slightly more aggressive, and instead
of waiting around for things to come your way, you may decide to grab
what you want with both hands. This might not be typical behaviour but
you can use it to your advantage.

24 THURSDAY
Moon Age Day 7   Moon Sign Virgo

am . . . .

pm . . . .
You never know when situations are going to turn your way and that is
especially the case at the moment. It's worth keeping your eyes open
because there are ways in which you can push ahead and get something
you have wanted for ages. Personal attachments look particularly good,
and you warm to the overtures of a specific individual.

25 FRIDAY
Moon Age Day 8   Moon Sign Virgo

am . . . .

pm . . . .
You needn't let any increase in work pressure disturb your equilibrium at this time, particularly if part of your mind is fully committed to matters that lie well beyond the scope of work and responsibility. The dreamy side of Cancer is showing but don't worry because this is one of the qualities of your nature that makes you so fascinating.

26 SATURDAY
Moon Age Day 9   Moon Sign Virgo

am . . . .

pm . . . .
You might be quite amazed to discover just how popular you can make yourself today and all because you simply do what seems to be the right thing. People could well turn to you for advice and even if you don't really understand the problem you should be capable of solving it. It's heart-warming to feel so needed.

27 SUNDAY
Moon Age Day 10   Moon Sign Libra

am . . . .

pm . . . .
It is true that not everyone will have your best interests at heart right now, but once you are aware of the fact you can quietly act to put things right. Taking people to task is rarely your thing, and is especially distasteful under present planetary trends. A new vista of possible social opportunity is now right before your eyes.

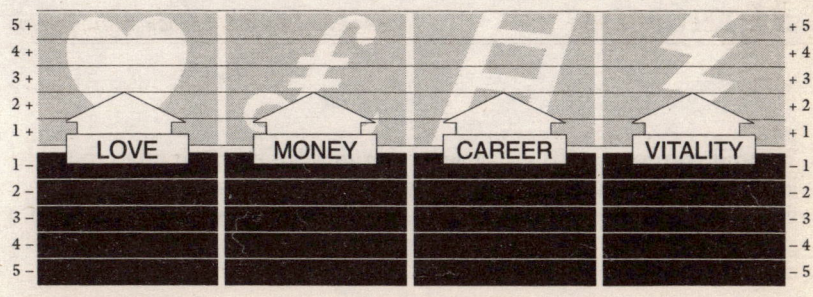

28 MONDAY
Moon Age Day 11   Moon Sign Libra

am . . . .

pm . . . .
You should have everything you need to move forward in a practical sense and the only thing that might be missing is your own motivation. This might be a pointer that something is wrong and that you are not finding the challenges you need the most. Your best response is to look at life again and do some rearranging.

29 TUESDAY
Moon Age Day 12   Moon Sign Scorpio

am . . . .

pm . . . .
Optimism and energy remain generally high, though it may be that not everyone seems to be offering the sort of support you might have come to expect. This could be because they have problems of their own about which you know nothing. Maybe a little gentle probing is in order, particularly if your curiosity is still at fever pitch!

30 WEDNESDAY
Moon Age Day 13   Moon Sign Scorpio

am . . . .

pm . . . .
Avoid the sort of mistakes that come from failing to pay enough attention to what you are doing. Concentration is now very important and especially so if you are dealing with subject matter you don't understand very well. Some romantic advantages could be there for the taking by this evening.

31 THURSDAY
Moon Age Day 14   Moon Sign Scorpio

am . . . .

pm . . . .
When it comes to solving problems you now have what it takes to be the best of the bunch. There are going to be a few obstacles to clear from your path today, but these should not present you with too much of a problem. Attitude is particularly important if you are dealing with family members who are less than happy.

1 FRIDAY
Moon Age Day 15   Moon Sign Sagittarius

am . . . .

pm . . . .
It's the start of a new month and you should be more than ready to cope with the various issues that life raises. In some ways you can afford to be more optimistic and happy with your lot than has been the case for a while. Workmates can be especially helpful at present, and could do much to lighten the load as far as you are concerned.

2 SATURDAY
Moon Age Day 16   Moon Sign Sagittarius

am . . . .

pm . . . .
The way forward is via excitement and originality, and you should make the most of these positive trends because by tomorrow the lunar low descends. It isn't like the Crab to act on impulse, but you have the potential to do so today. You can make sure that people are glad to have you around, even those you don't think are very fond of you.

3 SUNDAY
Moon Age Day 17   Moon Sign Capricorn

am . . . .

pm . . . .
Things could well slow quite noticeably, and even the easiest task could prove to be troublesome and without joy. As long as you understand that this is a very temporary state of affairs, you can ensure that all is well. What you can do today is to think things through and to plan ahead.

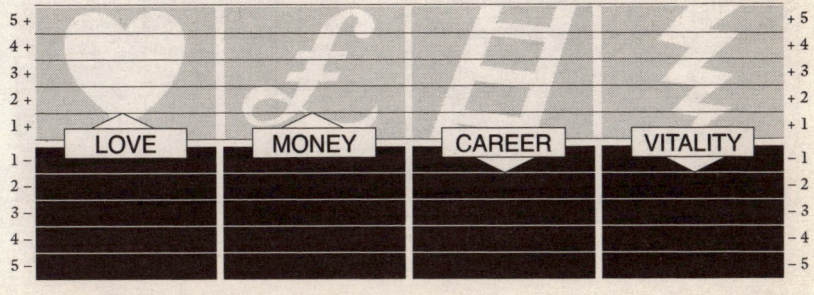

June 2007

YOUR MONTH AT A GLANCE

⊕ = Opportunities are around   ⊖ = Be on the defensive   ⬤ = Life is pretty ordinary

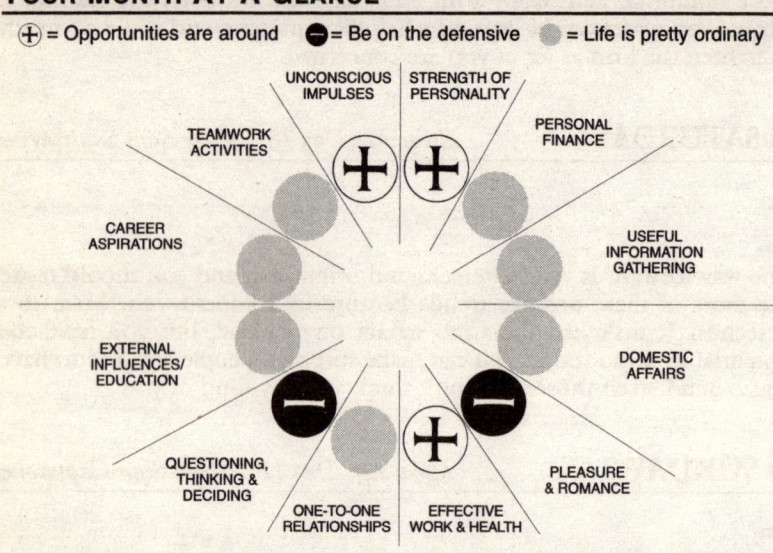

UNCONSCIOUS IMPULSES

STRENGTH OF PERSONALITY

TEAMWORK ACTIVITIES

PERSONAL FINANCE

CAREER ASPIRATIONS

USEFUL INFORMATION GATHERING

EXTERNAL INFLUENCES/ EDUCATION

DOMESTIC AFFAIRS

QUESTIONING, THINKING & DECIDING

ONE-TO-ONE RELATIONSHIPS

EFFECTIVE WORK & HEALTH

PLEASURE & ROMANCE

JUNE HIGHS AND LOWS

Here I show you how the rhythms of the Moon will affect you this month. Like the tide, your energies and abilities will rise and fall with its pattern. When it is above the centre line, go for it, when it is below, you should be resting.

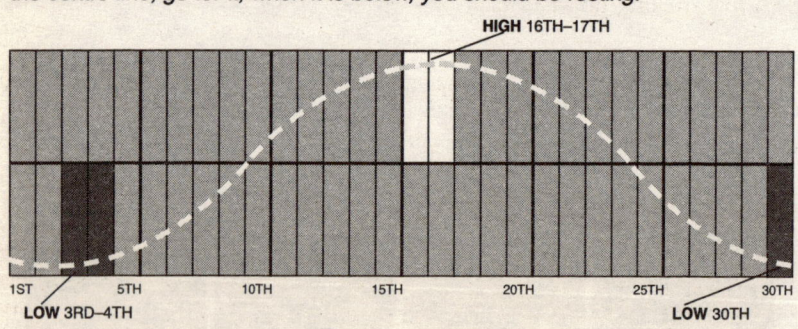

HIGH 16TH–17TH

1ST   5TH   10TH   15TH   20TH   25TH   30TH

LOW 3RD–4TH

LOW 30TH

4 MONDAY   *Moon Age Day 18   Moon Sign Capricorn*

am . . . .

pm . . . .
Even if you want to stir things up as far as your love life is concerned, maybe you should not try to do so right now. By tomorrow you can get right back on form again, but for the moment you are in recovery mode. Try not to be too quick to take offence with anyone who is really only trying to help you.

5 TUESDAY   *Moon Age Day 19   Moon Sign Aquarius*

am . . . .

pm . . . .
Today could be fairly unpredictable in some ways, but that isn't necessarily a bad thing. You have to react to situations and that makes you think in a slightly different way. The promised upturn in romantic possibilities comes along, though relationships generally may need a little nudge from you.

6 WEDNESDAY   *Moon Age Day 20   Moon Sign Aquarius*

am . . . .

pm . . . .
As far as work is concerned it seems that you have what it takes to cope with just about any challenge, and you may well be quite happy to take on something completely new. There is likely to be a good deal of excitement available under present astrological trends, though there may be a few sticking points too.

7 THURSDAY   *Moon Age Day 21   Moon Sign Aquarius*

am . . . .

pm . . . .
Could it be that the Crab is too impulsive for its own good at the moment? That is the way things look, so some extra care may be called for. Making arrangements for travel could be good, even if the journey itself is not to take place for quite some time. Don't be too quick to jump at what looks like a bargain, because it probably isn't!

8 FRIDAY
Moon Age Day 22   Moon Sign Pisces

am . . . .

pm . . . .
You need to make allowance in your thinking for the fact that some situations may not turn out the way you might have expected. Once again a reactive rather than proactive approach is best, and this can occasionally cause a slight problem. In the main you should be quite happy with your domestic and personal life.

9 SATURDAY
Moon Age Day 23   Moon Sign Pisces

am . . . .

pm . . . .
Bear in mind that not everyone is going to come up with the goods when you expect them to, and so there might be a few jobs you will have to do yourself if you want to be sure they are undertaken properly. This could see you jumping around from pillar to post today, but if your energy levels are high, all should be well.

10 SUNDAY
Moon Age Day 24   Moon Sign Aries

am . . . .

pm . . . .
Trends indicate that some new projects will have to wait if you are busy dealing with issues you see as being crucially important. Don't be afraid to seek help from friends and to get them to take some of the strain. Members of your family might be less obliging and even quite awkward on occasion.

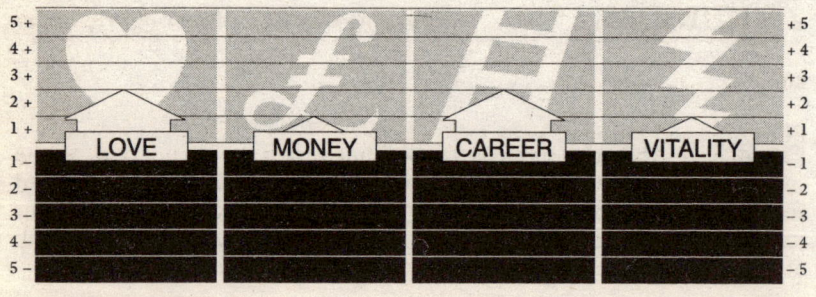

11 MONDAY   *Moon Age Day 25   Moon Sign Aries*

am . . . .

pm . . . .
Thoughts of romance are apt to fill your mind and the dreamy side of
Cancer may be much in evidence right now. All thoughts of practical jobs
can be out of the window as you seek to chase one or two dreams. Don't
worry about these trends because it is very important to look for the end
of the odd rainbow.

12 TUESDAY   *Moon Age Day 26   Moon Sign Taurus*

am . . . .

pm . . . .
The planetary picture changes slightly and this encourages you to be
more mentally alert and quite determined to do whatever is necessary to
finalise projects that have probably been waiting too long. Even if you
can't get colleagues to pull their weight, you have what it takes to find
ways and means to make significant progress.

13 WEDNESDAY   *Moon Age Day 27   Moon Sign Taurus*

am . . . .

pm . . . .
A time to trust your hunches and go down roads that seem logical to
you, even if those around you have some doubts. Your intuition is
highlighted at this time and you are unlikely to be misled by it. At the
same time it is important to avoid falling out with those very people who
are in the best position to help you. Diplomacy is called for.

14 THURSDAY   *Moon Age Day 28   Moon Sign Gemini*

am . . . .

pm . . . .
Things could slow down just a little, particularly if you are more
contemplative and inclined to withdraw into yourself somewhat. Mental
pursuits suit you so this may be a day for the crosswords and the sudoku.
Cancerians are usually big readers, and you may well have your nose stuck
into a book at every opportunity right now.

15 FRIDAY

Moon Age Day 0   Moon Sign Gemini

am . . . .

pm . . . .
Getting to grips with life may not seem too appealing, and at the end of
what has been a busy week you might decide you are happy to coast for
a few hours. Stand by for the opportunity for a rapid change in pace
because the lunar high is just around the corner. The weekend ahead
offers a fast and furious pace.

16 SATURDAY

Moon Age Day 1   Moon Sign Cancer

am . . . .

pm . . . .
It looks as though you can get Lady Luck on your side today. With little
time for the mundane or the ordinary you need to find new things to do
and will be seeking excitement. This might mean pushing others into
doing things they don't really fancy, but your powers of persuasion are
almost legendary at the moment.

17 SUNDAY

Moon Age Day 2   Moon Sign Cancer

am . . . .

pm . . . .
Getting your ideas across to others might not be so easy today, mainly
because the goal posts are shifting all the time. Even if you are still very
much in charge of your life and enjoying yourself, there can be small
frustrations when it seems impossible to get someone quite as motivated
as you are.

	LOVE	MONEY	CAREER	VITALITY
5 +				+ 5
4 +				+ 4
3 +				+ 3
2 +				+ 2
1 +				+ 1
1 -				- 1
2 -				- 2
3 -				- 3
4 -				- 4
5 -				- 5

18 MONDAY   *Moon Age Day 3   Moon Sign Leo*

am . . . .

pm . . . .
It's the start of another working week and trends encourage you to feel quite happy about most aspects of life. There may not be the same sense of excitement about that has perpetuated for the last couple of days, but on the other hand you are steadier and better able to grasp the significance of apparently small happenings.

19 TUESDAY   *Moon Age Day 4   Moon Sign Leo*

am . . . .

pm . . . .
The position of Venus in your solar chart offers a definite lift in one-to-one relationships. It's possible that love will come knocking on your door, and though this may seem rather inconvenient on what is otherwise a fairly busy Tuesday, it's good to know that you are top of the chart in someone's estimation.

20 WEDNESDAY   *Moon Age Day 5   Moon Sign Leo*

am . . . .

pm . . . .
It looks as though the Crab is in the mood for some spring cleaning. It isn't merely your house that requires a bit of a lift but the very essence of your life as a whole. There may be elements you simply want to dump, in favour of a new way of thinking and acting. Go slow at first or you will confuse those you depend upon.

21 THURSDAY   *Moon Age Day 6   Moon Sign Virgo*

am . . . .

pm . . . .
When it comes to social matters you can make this a very positive period. Don't stick around the same people all the time but rather do what you can to form new alliances and to get on side with people who have attracted you from a distance. There could be lots of personalities about at this time, and they fascinate you.

22 FRIDAY

Moon Age Day 7   Moon Sign Virgo

am . . . .

pm . . . .
Trends suggest that there is much in life that fascinates you right now and
that you want to discover the ins and outs of everything. This curiosity
turns out to be very important because you can make definite gains as a
result of it. You would be wise to avoid family rows under present trends
and rather be the peacemaker if at all possible.

23 SATURDAY

Moon Age Day 8   Moon Sign Libra

am . . . .

pm . . . .
Once again it seems you are inspired to make changes to the basic
structure of your life and the way you live it. If family and friends are
demanding your attention, there might not be quite as much time as you
would wish to please yourself, but you should be able to do your thinking
quite adequately whilst you are on the move.

24 SUNDAY

Moon Age Day 9   Moon Sign Libra

am . . . .

pm . . . .
You now have scope to expand your circle of contacts and to push the
bounds of the possible in some ways. The Crab is very diplomatic at the
best of times but rarely more so than turns out to be the case at the
moment. You can afford to push your luck a little more than usual.

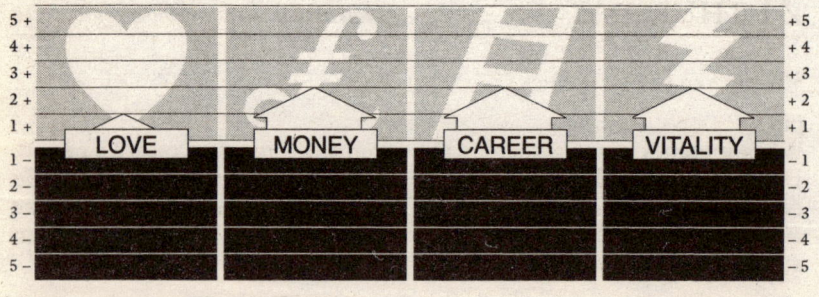

25 MONDAY
Moon Age Day 10   Moon Sign Libra

am . . . .

pm . . . .
What you can really put across at the moment is just how great your ego is. This could be a surprise to both you and the people in your immediate vicinity. The Crab doesn't always have a very high opinion of itself or its abilities, so it's refreshing to discover that you are capable of being both proud and pushy.

26 TUESDAY
Moon Age Day 11   Moon Sign Scorpio

am . . . .

pm . . . .
When it comes to getting the good things of life it looks as though you should be in a pretty good position right now. These trends are moderate so it's unlikely that you would suddenly scoop the jackpot on the National Lottery, but in small ways you do have what it takes to get ahead. Off the cuff gestures by others can be quite disarming.

27 WEDNESDAY
Moon Age Day 12   Moon Sign Scorpio

am . . . .

pm . . . .
If there is any chance at all for you to get away from the everyday routines of life today, don't be afraid to grab the possibility with both hands. Cancer could well be in the mood for travel and for pushing convention somewhat. This is easier for you to achieve far from home, so those of you who are on holiday are especially lucky.

28 THURSDAY
Moon Age Day 13   Moon Sign Sagittarius

am . . . .

pm . . . .
There could be some intimate issues that require a little attention today and that may lead to a real heart-to-heart with your partner or sweetheart. Don't worry if you can't make yourself fully understood because with a little patience all round you can make sure that things work out just fine.

29 FRIDAY
Moon Age Day 14   Moon Sign Sagittarius

am . . . .

pm . . . .
A boost to the level of your optimism is available to you immediately ahead of the lunar low. Today has potential to be quick-paced and in some ways fascinating, in stark contrast to what could come along tomorrow. For the moment you don't have to accept second-best from either yourself or others.

30 SATURDAY
Moon Age Day 15   Moon Sign Capricorn

am . . . .

pm . . . .
Any frustrations that surface right now come at least partly because the Moon is in your opposite zodiac sign of Capricorn. Your mind may not work as quickly as has been the case across the last week or so, and you could also find it difficult to deal with others and to get them to see things your way.

1 SUNDAY
☿ *Moon Age Day 16   Moon Sign Capricorn*

am . . . .

pm . . . .
The best way forward today is to alter your routines, even if this seems the last thing you really want to do. Of course you need quiet periods and the lunar low offers these, but there are a number of strong planetary influences encouraging you to push forward at the same time. Change and diversity suit the present astrological scene.

	LOVE		MONEY		CAREER		VITALITY	
5 +									+ 5
4 +									+ 4
3 +									+ 3
2 +									+ 2
1 +									+ 1
1 -									- 1
2 -									- 2
3 -									- 3
4 -									- 4
5 -									- 5

July 2007

YOUR MONTH AT A GLANCE

⊕ = Opportunities are around ⊖ = Be on the defensive ⬤ = Life is pretty ordinary

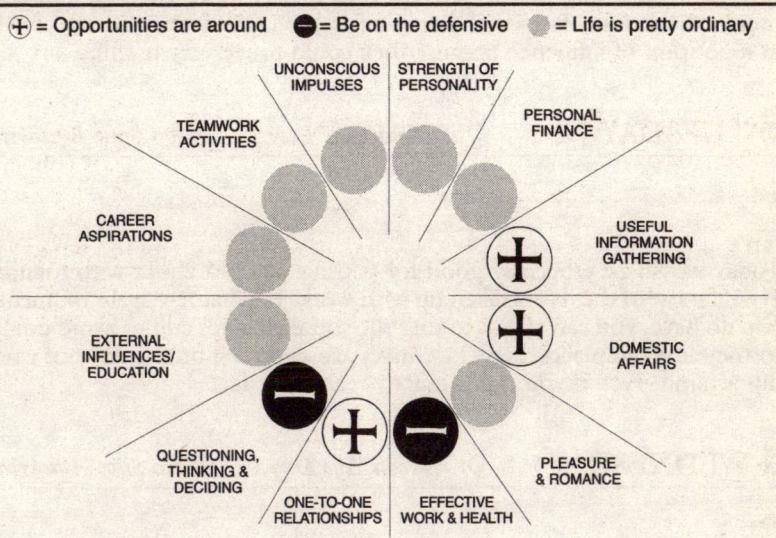

UNCONSCIOUS IMPULSES

STRENGTH OF PERSONALITY

PERSONAL FINANCE

TEAMWORK ACTIVITIES

USEFUL INFORMATION GATHERING

CAREER ASPIRATIONS

DOMESTIC AFFAIRS

EXTERNAL INFLUENCES/ EDUCATION

QUESTIONING, THINKING & DECIDING

PLEASURE & ROMANCE

ONE-TO-ONE RELATIONSHIPS

EFFECTIVE WORK & HEALTH

JULY HIGHS AND LOWS

Here I show you how the rhythms of the Moon will affect you this month. Like the tide, your energies and abilities will rise and fall with its pattern. When it is above the centre line, go for it, when it is below, you should be resting.

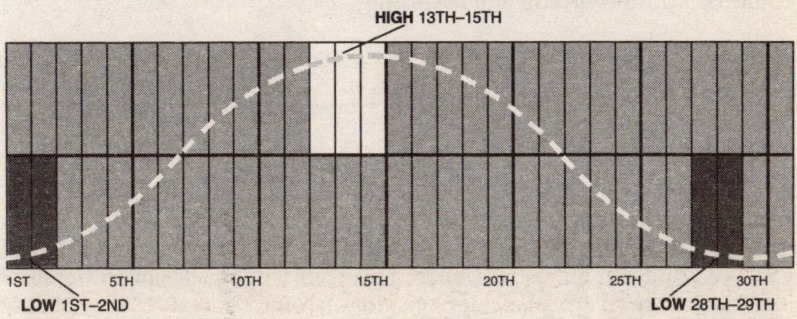

HIGH 13TH–15TH

1ST   5TH   10TH   15TH   20TH   25TH   30TH

LOW 1ST–2ND

LOW 28TH–29TH

2 MONDAY ☿ *Moon Age Day 17 Moon Sign Capricorn*

am . . . .

pm . . . .
Why not put your charm to the test at the start of this week? Although the lunar low remains around for the first few hours of the day, it shouldn't take long before you are able to feel more cheerful and also more mischievous. It's worth keeeping well on side with someone who is in a position of influence because they could prove very useful.

3 TUESDAY ☿ *Moon Age Day 18 Moon Sign Aquarius*

am . . . .

pm . . . .
Today would be especially good for getting out and about with friends, even if most of the day is taken up with work. In what few spare moments you do have, you can afford to ring the social changes and to avoid going to the same old places. New incentives are knocking on the door of your inner mind, even if you don't exactly realise the fact.

4 WEDNESDAY ☿ *Moon Age Day 19 Moon Sign Aquarius*

am . . . .

pm . . . .
Meetings can be made fun, even if they are really about work. You know how to wring humour out of any situation at the moment and can be centre-stage in a way that would sometimes make you feel slightly uncomfortable. The romantic responses you can attract from others could be both rewarding and surprising.

5 THURSDAY ☿ *Moon Age Day 20 Moon Sign Pisces*

am . . . .

pm . . . .
Even if business has to come before pleasure today, that needn't be too much of a problem because you can mix and match both at present. The Crab can find fun almost anywhere and your laughter is apt to be quite infectious. There are planetary positions around you now that simply enhance your happiness.

6 FRIDAY ☿ *Moon Age Day 21   Moon Sign Pisces*

am . . . .

pm . . . .
Don't be afraid to look for some relaxation and make the most of it when
it does come along. This doesn't necessarily mean doing nothing but just
things that are different from your normal work and domestic routines.
Someone you have always thought of as being distinctly cool may now
surprise and amuse you.

7 SATURDAY ☿ *Moon Age Day 22   Moon Sign Aries*

am . . . .

pm . . . .
This would be one of the best days of the month during which to get
involved in new cultural projects and a period for proving to yourself and
the world how intellectual you really are. You may decide to leave a few
routine jobs on the shelf, but if you are really lucky someone else might
deal with them in any case.

8 SUNDAY ☿ *Moon Age Day 23   Moon Sign Aries*

am . . . .

pm . . . .
When it comes to expanding your horizons, present trends simply could
not be better. You can be a real optimist at the moment and can achieve
things that would prove to be very difficult for you as a rule. You needn't
take no for an answer if you are certain in your own mind that you see
the future very clearly.

5 +			+ 5
4 +			+ 4
3 +			+ 3
2 +			+ 2
1 +			+ 1
LOVE	MONEY	CAREER	VITALITY
1 –			– 1
2 –			– 2
3 –			– 3
4 –			– 4
5 –			– 5

9 MONDAY ☿ *Moon Age Day 24 Moon Sign Taurus*

am . . . .

pm . . . .
Another favourable day for widening your vision. You can take this opportunity to get rid of outmoded concepts and to look forward very positively. The only slight drawback today could be if someone else holds you back, possibly for purely selfish reasons.

10 TUESDAY ☿ *Moon Age Day 25 Moon Sign Taurus*

am . . . .

pm . . . .
You have scope to obtain assistance when you need it the most today, perhaps from some expected directions as well as more unlikely ones. Don't be too quick to take the initiative regarding any issue that is going to mean a great deal of work for very little reward. Let someone else have the privilege for once!

11 WEDNESDAY *Moon Age Day 26 Moon Sign Gemini*

am . . . .

pm . . . .
It may be best to keep to tried and tested paths, at least for today and tomorrow. The inspirational Crab comes along on Friday, but for the moment you would be better or not pushing your luck or your physique too much. This may not even be an issue, particularly if you are in a mood that responds to relaxation.

12 THURSDAY *Moon Age Day 27 Moon Sign Gemini*

am . . . .

pm . . . .
There are times when you can surprise yourself with your simple genius. Whilst others may be flapping around and putting masses of effort into life, you have what it takes to run a lot of it by virtual remote control today. Cancer is in a meditative state of mind and that enables you to become even more attractive to certain people.

13 FRIDAY

Moon Age Day 28   Moon Sign Cancer

am . . . .

pm . . . .
The lunar high inclines you to be anxious to get on and probably slightly lacking in patience with those who simply don't understand what you are saying. You might simply decide to leave them behind for the moment because dynamism is everything and there probably isn't time to explain yourself at every turn.

14 SATURDAY

Moon Age Day 29   Moon Sign Cancer

am . . . .

pm . . . .
With everything to play for and the level of general luck probably better than it has been for a number of weeks, this is the time during July when you can make the world your oyster. It seems as if time is like elastic because you have the ability to get so much done, particularly with the invaluable support of friends.

15 SUNDAY

Moon Age Day 0   Moon Sign Cancer

am . . . .

pm . . . .
The positive trends should continue today but might display themselves in a slightly different way. What you need now is to have a good time, and in order to fulfil this desire you may decide to lay down some of the ordinary responsibilities of life. A day to find something to do that pleases you but which also stretches your capabilities.

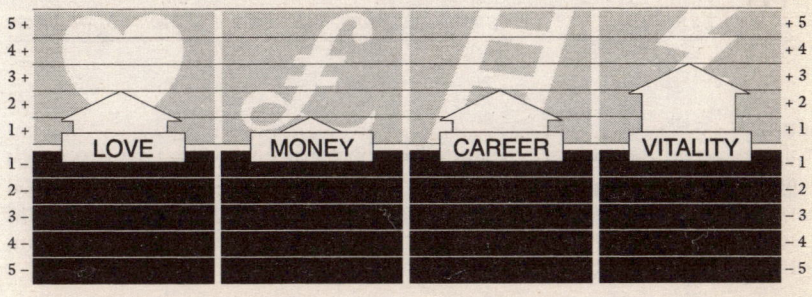

16 MONDAY
Moon Age Day 1   Moon Sign Leo

am . . . .

pm . . . .
Whatever you are doing today, you have the ability to bring a sense of harmony to life. A slower pace is possible, but it is one of your choosing and not something that is foisted upon you by circumstance. Understanding the way the world works seems to be child's play for you, even if it confuses your friends at the moment.

17 TUESDAY
Moon Age Day 2   Moon Sign Leo

am . . . .

pm . . . .
Trends enhance your mental powers, and someone would have to get out of bed very early in the day if they wanted to fool you in any way. The same probably cannot be said for your partner or a relative. Much of what is good about this period is being able to direct other people along a wiser and safer path.

18 WEDNESDAY
Moon Age Day 3   Moon Sign Virgo

am . . . .

pm . . . .
Don't be afraid to take good ideas and to act on them, especially where your work is concerned. You have what it takes to simplify issues that others are making unnecessarily complicated and you won't do yourself any harm on the way. If people are watching you at present, make sure they like what they see.

19 THURSDAY
Moon Age Day 4   Moon Sign Virgo

am . . . .

pm . . . .
There could be a slight tendency for you to dwell on the past too much and that is something you should try to avoid under present astrological trends. It could well take a great determination to cast your mind forward in time and to still the waves of nostalgia that come over you, but the effort should be rewarded.

20 FRIDAY
Moon Age Day 5   Moon Sign Libra

am . . . .

pm . . . .
You can be at your most persuasive on this summer Friday, and might prove to be so charming that it is doubtful that anyone would deny you your way. With your sense of humour highlighted at present, you can make everyone laugh and bring a breath of fresh air to just about any situation in which you are involved.

21 SATURDAY
Moon Age Day 6   Moon Sign Libra

am . . . .

pm . . . .
Those Crabs who work on a Saturday might have the best of the trends today, but that doesn't mean a bad time for any of you. It is simply the case that your mind is now especially well tuned towards professional and practical issues for the moment. You should quickly be able to dispel any thought of sitting around and doing nothing.

22 SUNDAY
Moon Age Day 7   Moon Sign Libra

am . . . .

pm . . . .
General progress is possible, no matter where you turn your mind at this time. Everyday routines could appear quite tedious and you operate best when you can ring the changes and when you insist on doing things your own way. It's worth keeping in touch with friends right now and especially those at a distance.

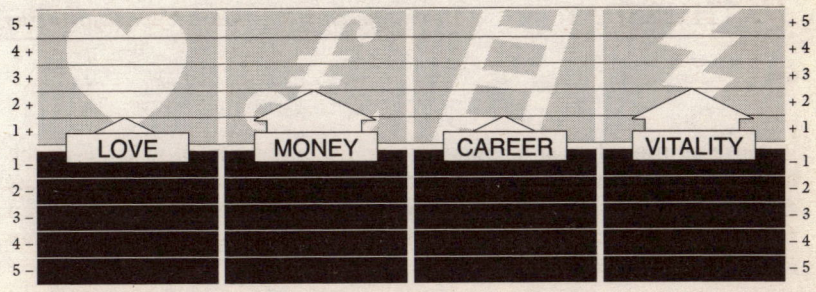

23 MONDAY
Moon Age Day 8   Moon Sign Scorpio

am . . . .

pm . . . .
Diplomacy is your middle name and this could prove to be especially fortunate at the start of this working week. Even if others find it difficult to see the bigger picture and to operate without being reactive, you are able to calm almost any situation. This is a gift and is one that a few of those with whom you are associated should envy.

24 TUESDAY
Moon Age Day 9   Moon Sign Scorpio

am . . . .

pm . . . .
Trends assist you to pluck solutions out of the mist and once again to show your ability to sort things out whilst your colleagues or friends are flapping around. In some ways this might increase your popularity but don't expect everyone to be grateful. Just carry on in that calm and happy Cancerian way.

25 WEDNESDAY
Moon Age Day 10   Moon Sign Sagittarius

am . . . .

pm . . . .
There could be minor financial gains possible around but these are not likely to be great in scale. Perhaps you are now simply better at looking ahead and making the right monetary choices. Don't get bogged down in discussions that lead nowhere, and if you see a logjam developing, do your best to sort it out.

26 THURSDAY
Moon Age Day 11   Moon Sign Sagittarius

am . . . .

pm . . . .
It looks as though you are on a perpetual quest for knowledge at the moment and you will not be content until you find an answer for almost everything. This is not typical behaviour for your zodiac sign and so you might surprise yourself, especially with your present tenacity. Why not try to relax later in the day?

27 FRIDAY *Moon Age Day 12   Moon Sign Sagittarius*

am . . . .

pm . . . .
This will be a really good day for seeing just how popular you are and for reaping the rewards of efforts you have put in previously. Even if family members prove to be quite demanding, you can take their needs in your stride and would be unlikely to lose your temper whilst present planetary trends continue.

28 SATURDAY *Moon Age Day 13   Moon Sign Capricorn*

am . . . .

pm . . . .
This may not be the most positive or eventful weekend of the year, but the fact shouldn't worry you in the slightest. The lunar low represents a time to rest and to think ahead and is not an opportunity to push yourself to the limit. Try for a steady sort of day and allow others to take some of the strain in a domestic sense.

29 SUNDAY *Moon Age Day 14   Moon Sign Capricorn*

am . . . .

pm . . . .
You want to see results from your efforts, but may have to realise that some of these are going to come a little further down the line. As long as you do not have too many great expectations you can make this a settled and generally contented interval, but it is probably not a time for pushing your luck too far.

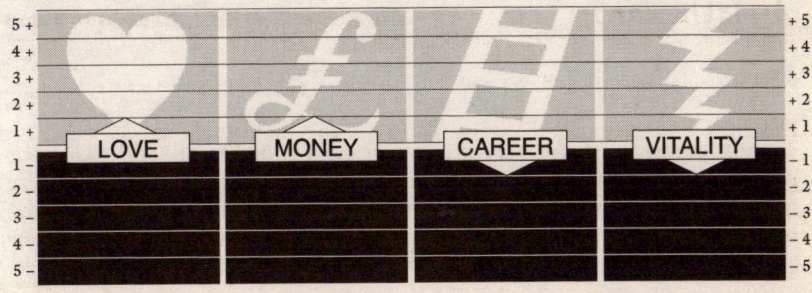

30 MONDAY   *Moon Age Day 15   Moon Sign Aquarius*

am . . . .

pm . . . .
Social relationships are likely to be well accented now, encouraging you to turn your attention towards a greater mixing and mingling with the world at large this week. With the lunar low out of the way finances should look slightly better and you may decide to splash out on something you have wanted for a while.

31 TUESDAY   *Moon Age Day 16   Moon Sign Aquarius*

am . . . .

pm . . . .
Don't miss out on any opportunity today. It is professional matters that fall under the spotlight, even though personal attachments also have a strong part to play in your present thinking. If you get the opportunity to step into the limelight later in the day, don't allow your natural shyness to get in the way.

1 WEDNESDAY   *Moon Age Day 17   Moon Sign Pisces*

am . . . .

pm . . . .
It is the start of a new month and you can afford to feel very hopeful. Not everything is going to turn out exactly as you might wish, but you are very good at thinking on your feet and can make necessary changes on the way. It isn't so much the destinations that matter at present but rather the enjoyment of the journey.

2 THURSDAY   *Moon Age Day 18   Moon Sign Pisces*

am . . . .

pm . . . .
Trends suggest you are very incisive in your judgements and that your comments go straight to the heart of most matters. This is a quality others lack and one or two people may be slightly envious of you at the moment. Rather than reacting to provocation, why not turn your attention towards people who are relaxed and happy?

3 FRIDAY
Moon Age Day 19   Moon Sign Aries

am . . . .

pm . . . .
The generosity of spirit displayed by the zodiac sign of Cancer is positively legendary and it seems as though you would move the world sideways to help anyone at the present time. You can't expect the whole world to fully appreciate your positive gestures, but you can carry on lending a hand all the same.

4 SATURDAY
Moon Age Day 20   Moon Sign Aries

am . . . .

pm . . . .
A few demanding issues might well put you to the test today, and how you rise to the situation might be being carefully monitored by others. There may not be time for quite as much social diversion as you would wish at the start of this weekend, but you are able to make headway with something you see as being very important.

5 SUNDAY
Moon Age Day 21   Moon Sign Taurus

am . . . .

pm . . . .
Good luck is there for the taking as a result of travel and Crabs who have decided on this week to take a holiday could be the luckiest of all. Nevertheless, even if you can only find the time to take a walk around your local park, you gain from getting away from the everyday associations of life.

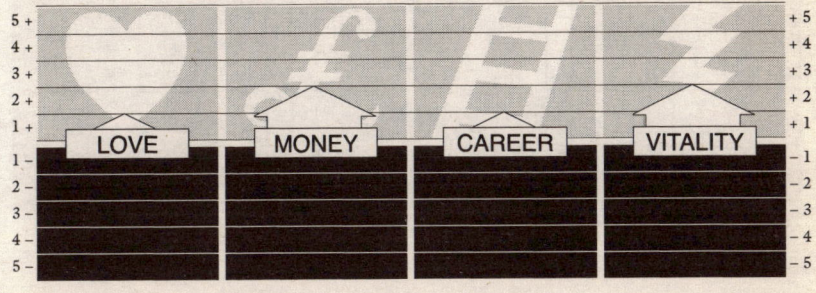

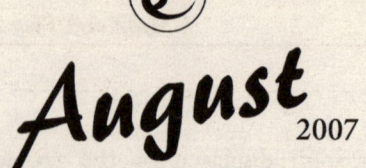

August 2007

YOUR MONTH AT A GLANCE

⊕ = Opportunities are around   ⊖ = Be on the defensive   ⬤ = Life is pretty ordinary

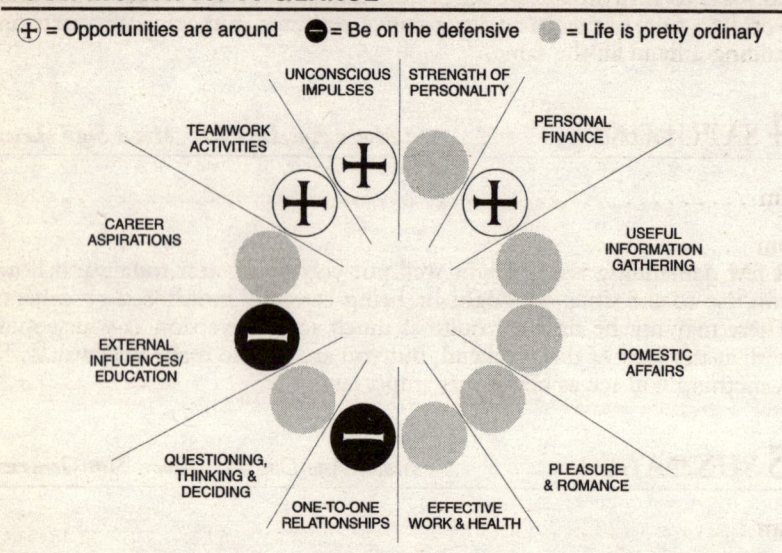

UNCONSCIOUS IMPULSES
STRENGTH OF PERSONALITY
PERSONAL FINANCE
TEAMWORK ACTIVITIES
CAREER ASPIRATIONS
USEFUL INFORMATION GATHERING
EXTERNAL INFLUENCES/ EDUCATION
DOMESTIC AFFAIRS
QUESTIONING, THINKING & DECIDING
PLEASURE & ROMANCE
ONE-TO-ONE RELATIONSHIPS
EFFECTIVE WORK & HEALTH

AUGUST HIGHS AND LOWS

Here I show you how the rhythms of the Moon will affect you this month. Like the tide, your energies and abilities will rise and fall with its pattern. When it is above the centre line, go for it, when it is below, you should be resting.

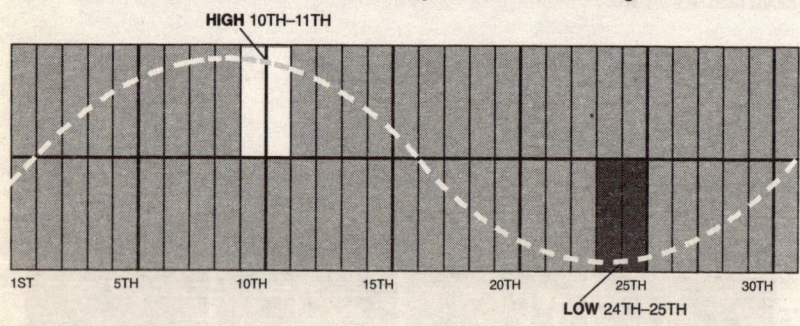

HIGH 10TH–11TH

LOW 24TH–25TH

1ST   5TH   10TH   15TH   20TH   25TH   30TH

6 MONDAY   *Moon Age Day 22   Moon Sign Taurus*

am . . . .

pm . . . .
Trends assist you to be friendly and very communicative today. Now would be as good a time as any to seek advancement of some sort and to ask for favours. You can use your sweet nature to attract positive attention from the world at large and you could find that even strangers seem to be especially helpful.

7 TUESDAY   *Moon Age Day 23   Moon Sign Taurus*

am . . . .

pm . . . .
Social relationships remain potentially excellent, even if there are one or two of your friends who seem to be behaving in a less than typical manner. By all means give yourself a pat on the back for something that is turning out more or less the way you have wished, but don't slacken your pace in terms of ambitions.

8 WEDNESDAY   *Moon Age Day 24   Moon Sign Gemini*

am . . . .

pm . . . .
You can probably afford to slow down a bit today, and in any case with the present position of the Moon the dreamier side of your nature pays a visit. It's just as important to plan as to do, which is probably just as well under present trends. You continue to be able to obtain help and advice from those around you.

9 THURSDAY   *Moon Age Day 25   Moon Sign Gemini*

am . . . .

pm . . . .
There will be no doubting your generosity at present but you can be too giving and this is not the way to be, particularly with younger family members. You must allow others to stand on their own feet, and in any case you need to feed your own need for rest and relaxation today.

10 FRIDAY

Moon Age Day 26   Moon Sign Cancer

am . . . .

pm . . . .
The lunar high offers new incentives and helps you to bring excitement into your life. Where things are slow you now have what it takes to speed up the pace of life and you show a willing and happy attitude to the world. Conforming to the expectations of others is now a piece of cake, even if you are really doing your own thing.

11 SATURDAY

Moon Age Day 27   Moon Sign Cancer

am . . . .

pm . . . .
The positive trends continue and today would be excellent for getting out of the house and doing something exciting. Not everything you undertake at the moment has to have a tangible result, because the successes come in any case. Good company, good food and good times should all appeal at the moment.

12 SUNDAY

Moon Age Day 28   Moon Sign Leo

am . . . .

pm . . . .
There could well be a few demanding issues to deal with now and one or two of these might put you to the test. This is no bad thing, because you have to stretch you capabilities from time to time. You need change and diversity under present trends – all the better if you have opted for a holiday at this time.

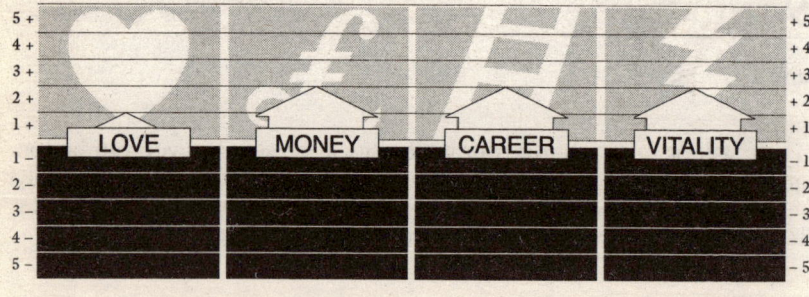

13 MONDAY

Moon Age Day 0   Moon Sign Leo

am . . . .

pm . . . .
Now is the time to be broadening your horizons, which is why you might decide to try something new. With the help of the planet Mars you can use this interlude to improve your fitness and stamina, and one option is to take up some new form of exercise or physical activity.

14 TUESDAY

Moon Age Day 1   Moon Sign Virgo

am . . . .

pm . . . .
One or two problems from the past have potential to surface around now. Instead of putting these back into the cupboard of your mind it would be worthwhile sorting them out once and for all. In a social sense you may feel a need to ring the changes – a trend that recurs frequently under current influences.

15 WEDNESDAY

Moon Age Day 2   Moon Sign Virgo

am . . . .

pm . . . .
The signs are that anything that makes you feel more alive and in charge will appeal today. You won't mind sorting out minute details if that is what it takes to get ahead, and you also have the right knack of persuading colleagues to do what you would wish. You would be wise to avoid getting into a family row that has no real purpose.

16 THURSDAY

Moon Age Day 3   Moon Sign Virgo

am . . . .

pm . . . .
There could well be a slight tendency for you to be irritable at the moment, but if you realise that this is the case, there is a chance you can prevent yourself from going too far. You certainly know what you want at present, even if circumstances prevent you from achieving some of your objectives.

17 FRIDAY
Moon Age Day 4   Moon Sign Libra

am . . . .

pm . . . .
You can allow your self-confidence to increase significantly as the Moon enters the zodiac sign of Libra, throwing a positive light on other planets in your solar chart. You have scope to show yourself to be articulate and even quite powerful, and to adopt an attitude that could surprise anyone who thinks you are a shrinking violet.

18 SATURDAY
Moon Age Day 5   Moon Sign Libra

am . . . .

pm . . . .
Even the most casual conversations can prove to be grist to the mill as far as your active and enterprising mind is concerned. If you still don't have all your accustomed patience, it would be sensible to avoid mixing too much with people you can't help thinking are idiots. The Crab remains determined and single-minded.

19 SUNDAY
Moon Age Day 6   Moon Sign Scorpio

am . . . .

pm . . . .
You need to make favourable contacts with others right now if you are going to get the most out of life. This is no time to be hanging around in the shadows, and would be an excellent interlude to get yourself fully involved in something quite new. Romance looks good under present planetary trends.

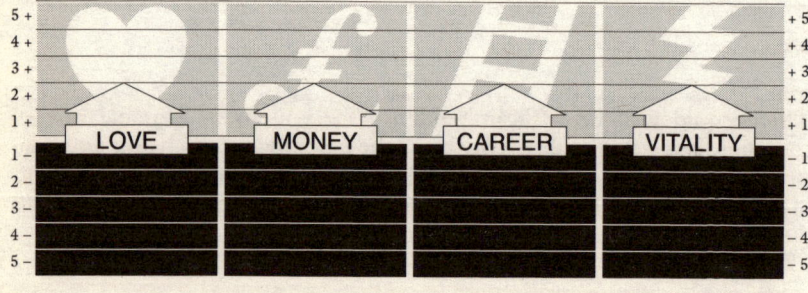

20 MONDAY
Moon Age Day 7   Moon Sign Scorpio

am . . . .

pm . . . .
Stand by for a potentially restless period and for a time during which you need to show a greater understanding of the way your own inner mind works. As a rule you are so busy offering assistance to others that you spend very little time getting to know what makes you tick. For at least today you can afford to be more self-indulgent.

21 TUESDAY
Moon Age Day 8   Moon Sign Scorpio

am . . . .

pm . . . .
Trends suggest you should be careful who you trust at present and especially so where money is concerned. There is just a chance that you might end up making some unwise financial decisions. All in all it would probably be better to keep your purse or wallet tightly closed, at least until tomorrow.

22 WEDNESDAY
Moon Age Day 9   Moon Sign Sagittarius

am . . . .

pm . . . .
Standard responses might not work too well at the moment and especially so if you are dealing with people who simply will not listen to what you are trying to say. Fortunately your mind is fertile and you can always think of a different way to approach a particular issue.

23 THURSDAY
Moon Age Day 10   Moon Sign Sagittarius

am . . . .

pm . . . .
Trends encourage you to put much of your energy now into group activities and funding new family projects. As is often the case, you may well put yourself second, in favour of supporting your nearest and dearest. There's nothing wrong with this, and it epitomizes the Crab, but you need to look to your own needs now and again.

24 FRIDAY
Moon Age Day 11   Moon Sign Capricorn

am . . . .

pm . . . .
A slower day is a distinct possibility, and one during which you probably won't be able to achieve your greatest objectives. However, if you turn your mind inward a little you can do plenty of planning. This is the way to beat the worst effects of the lunar low, and also gives you the chance to remain generally content.

25 SATURDAY
Moon Age Day 12   Moon Sign Capricorn

am . . . .

pm . . . .
Although you want to be positive today, it appears that opportunities are running like sand through your fingers. This is no time to panic. You can achieve the things you want in the end, but just not today. Rather than trying to knock your head against a wall, you should be willing to watch and wait.

26 SUNDAY
Moon Age Day 13   Moon Sign Aquarius

am . . . .

pm . . . .
Confidence returns very quickly once the Moon passes into Aquarius. Your strength today lies in the originality of your thinking. Whilst others are flogging themselves to death trying to do something in the same old way, you are able to look at life from a sideways angle and get ahead that much better.

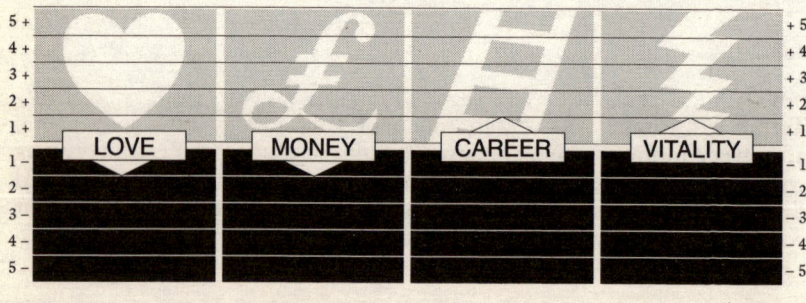

27 MONDAY *Moon Age Day 14   Moon Sign Aquarius*

am . . . .

pm . . . .
Stand by to make the most of a much luckier period and a time during which something you thought was lost forever once again becomes more than possible. Don't use up your energy chasing rainbows but rather concentrate on matters that have a strong practical quality. Romantic overtures could be noticeable by the evening.

28 TUESDAY *Moon Age Day 15   Moon Sign Aquarius*

am . . . .

pm . . . .
You may decide that there isn't much sense in spending too much money at present, particularly since most of what you really want in life comes free of charge. You may also have to curb the extravagant tendencies of younger family members, particularly if they think that money grows on the nearest tree!

29 WEDNESDAY *Moon Age Day 16   Moon Sign Pisces*

am . . . .

pm . . . .
They say that actions speak louder than words and this certainly seems to be the case for you at the moment. Although you can be the deepest and most contemplative of all the zodiac signs, this might be far from the case now. Now is the time to get on with life and keep as active as possible. You can obtain help if you need it.

30 THURSDAY *Moon Age Day 17   Moon Sign Pisces*

am . . . .

pm . . . .
How very innovative you can be at the present time! When you have a really ingenious idea you need to follow it to its logical conclusion. It shouldn't be hard for you to speak up in group situations or where your opinion is being sought at work. Look out for any chance to shine socially later in the day.

31 FRIDAY
Moon Age Day 18   Moon Sign Aries

am . . . .

pm . . . .
You might surprise others with your assertiveness today. It might appear as though you have taken some strange potion that has changed your nature almost totally, but all that has really happened is that the Moon has moved in your solar chart to a position that encourages a more aggressive attitude to life.

1 SATURDAY
Moon Age Day 19   Moon Sign Aries

am . . . .

pm . . . .
Creative potential remains good, but it is clear that your nature right now is quite complex and difficult for even you to understand. You can't really expect others to make sense of your present reasoning and actions if you don't comprehend them yourself, but all of this does at least make for an interesting interlude.

2 SUNDAY
Moon Age Day 20   Moon Sign Taurus

am . . . .

pm . . . .
Trends suggest that it is social matters and domestic matters that prove to be most heart-warming on this late summer Sunday. With a very practical attitude you could also be deciding on changes you want to make around your home and might decide that today is as good as any time to put them into practice.

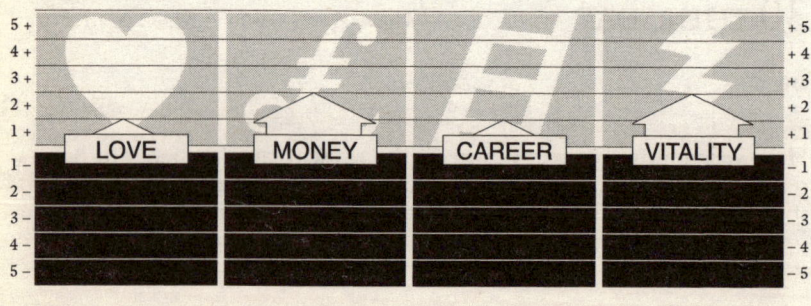

September 2007

YOUR MONTH AT A GLANCE

⊕ = Opportunities are around ⊖ = Be on the defensive ● = Life is pretty ordinary

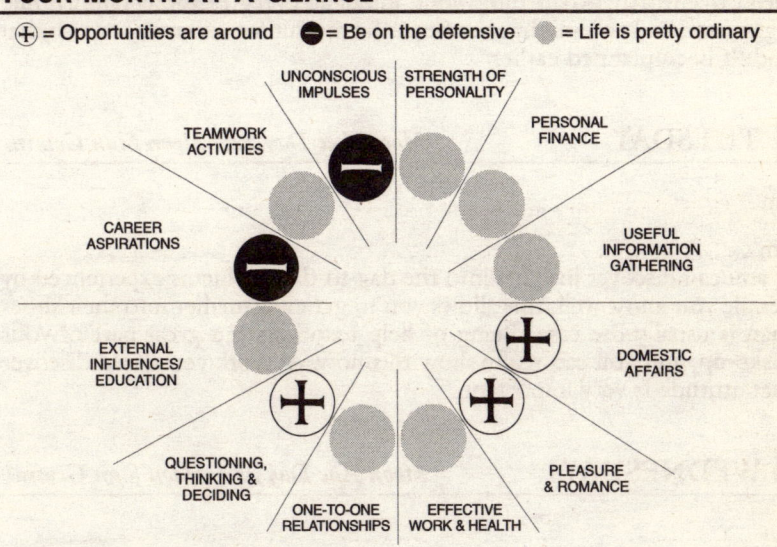

- UNCONSCIOUS IMPULSES ⊖
- STRENGTH OF PERSONALITY
- TEAMWORK ACTIVITIES
- PERSONAL FINANCE
- CAREER ASPIRATIONS ⊖
- USEFUL INFORMATION GATHERING
- EXTERNAL INFLUENCES/ EDUCATION
- DOMESTIC AFFAIRS ⊕
- QUESTIONING, THINKING & DECIDING ⊕
- ONE-TO-ONE RELATIONSHIPS
- EFFECTIVE WORK & HEALTH ⊕
- PLEASURE & ROMANCE

SEPTEMBER HIGHS AND LOWS

Here I show you how the rhythms of the Moon will affect you this month. Like the tide, your energies and abilities will rise and fall with its pattern. When it is above the centre line, go for it, when it is below, you should be resting.

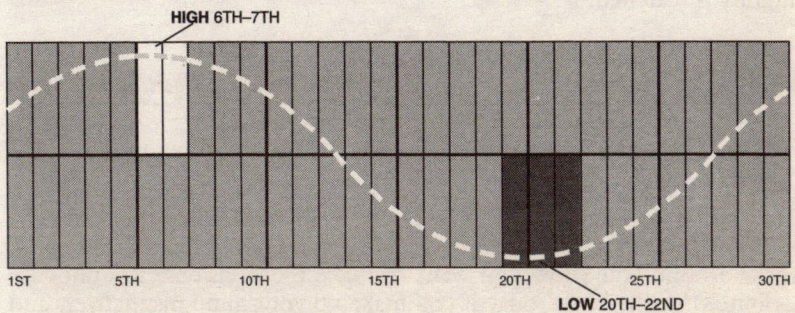

HIGH 6TH–7TH

LOW 20TH–22ND

1ST 5TH 10TH 15TH 20TH 25TH 30TH

3 MONDAY
Moon Age Day 21   Moon Sign Taurus

am . . . .

pm . . . .
Intimate relationships are especially favoured at present, at least partly because you can sense and understand the feelings of others particularly well. It's worth broadening your mind at every possible opportunity right now, and you might even be in the market for a journey or two that hadn't been planned earlier.

4 TUESDAY
Moon Age Day 22   Moon Sign Gemini

am . . . .

pm . . . .
If you can discover insights into the day-to-day problems experienced by people you know well, this allows you to get even further into their shoes than is usually the case. Being of help to others is a great part of your make-up, and you can really show this now. At work you could discover that attitude is very important.

5 WEDNESDAY
Moon Age Day 23   Moon Sign Gemini

am . . . .

pm . . . .
Your sense of security and peace of mind can be boosted by present planetary trends, and even if you show the quieter side of your nature on occasions today, in the main you can make life run fairly smoothly. Don't be too quick to crawl into your shell in the evening, just because you feel slightly threatened.

6 THURSDAY
Moon Age Day 24   Moon Sign Cancer

am . . . .

pm . . . .
Now you have what it takes to be out in front and leading the field. The lunar high offers you superior judgement and enough confidence to let those around you know you want to make the decisions. Routines are definitely for the birds today if you make up your mind instinctively and act very much on impulse.

7 FRIDAY
Moon Age Day 25   Moon Sign Cancer

am . . . .

pm . . . .

Many of your decisions appear to have lucky consequences at the moment. This is partly down to your actions but is also a response to the lunar high. There is a certain fluency to what you are doing and matters should seem far more connected than might sometimes be the case. A great time to mix business and pleasure.

8 SATURDAY
Moon Age Day 26   Moon Sign Leo

am . . . .

pm . . . .

A day to take care when handling personal encounters. Problems could arise if you are simply too busy to pay attention but also because of the present position of the planet Mars in your solar chart. Some extra care is necessary when dealing with a person who is definitely far too sensitive.

9 SUNDAY
Moon Age Day 27   Moon Sign Leo

am . . . .

pm . . . .

Friendly co-operation is worth a great deal at the moment and you have the chance to establish a better relationship with people who might have slightly intimidated you in the past. Maybe they have a greater need of you or are simply showing the more vulnerable side of their nature?

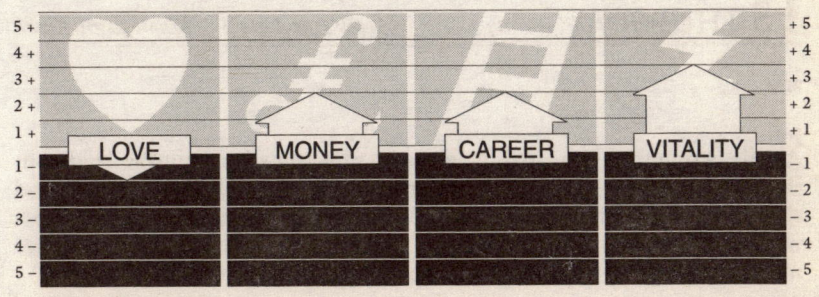

10 MONDAY
Moon Age Day 28   Moon Sign Leo

am . . . .

pm . . . .
The main sources of joy and pleasure coming into your life at the moment are friends and colleagues. From others you can gain entertainment and significant diversions from the mundane aspects of life. Social impulses are also well accented, offering you scope to mix as much as possible.

11 TUESDAY
Moon Age Day 29   Moon Sign Virgo

am . . . .

pm . . . .
Don't take anything for granted as far as close relationships are concerned. You might have to go over the top in terms of compliments in order to get your partner believing that you really do care, and this period of insecurity on their behalf can be slightly wearing to you. Younger family members could be a greater source of joy.

12 WEDNESDAY
Moon Age Day 0   Moon Sign Virgo

am . . . .

pm . . . .
As far as your list of priorities is concerned right now it looks as though you may be giving a great deal of your time and attention to purely practical matters. This might leave less available space to concentrate on either social matters or personal attachments. It's worth making a mental note to put this right later.

13 THURSDAY
Moon Age Day 1   Moon Sign Libra

am . . . .

pm . . . .
A little extra effort is probably necessary now in order to ensure that your plans are on target, but you can maintain a generally cheerful attitude and should be piling on the effort in jobs you really enjoy. Concern for those who have less than you remains to the fore, and your social conscience may be stronger than at any time for the last month or so.

14 FRIDAY
Moon Age Day 2   Moon Sign Libra

am . . . .

pm . . . .
Don't be afraid to keep on the move at the end of this working week and show those who count that you have what it takes to go solo in certain tasks. When away from work you can be witty and even quite sharp, factors that help you to get noticed. Romance is a distinct possibility for the weekend ahead, so why not plan something special today?

15 SATURDAY
Moon Age Day 3   Moon Sign Scorpio

am . . . .

pm . . . .
Trends now encourage you to renew and revitalise, and this is especially true when it comes to the way you see and handle personal attachments. Intuition should be especially strong, enabling you to see through situations that leave others confused. An ideal day to spend time with your partner or sweetheart and to pile on the compliments.

16 SUNDAY
Moon Age Day 4   Moon Sign Scorpio

am . . . .

pm . . . .
This ought to be a productive day and one during which you should be willing to make almost any change you see as necessary in order to get where you want to be in the near future. In terms of communication you can afford to be very direct and far more willing than usual to push your luck generally.

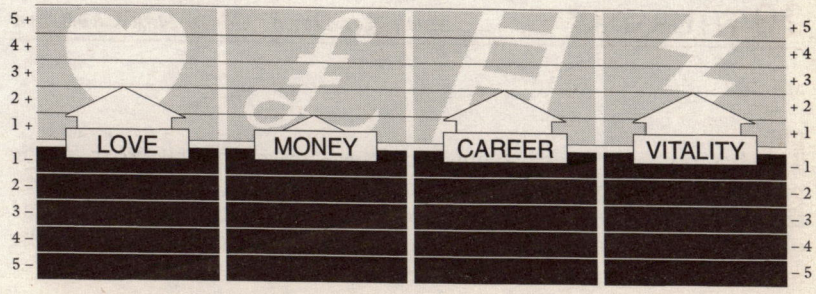

17 MONDAY

Moon Age Day 5   Moon Sign Scorpio

am . . . .

pm . . . .
Don't leave anything to chance today. It is important to check all details carefully and to be sure that you know what is expected of you under any given circumstance. A few potentially quieter days lie ahead later and so you would be wise to get anything out of the way that you know is vitally important. It's worth keeping abreast of local events.

18 TUESDAY

Moon Age Day 6   Moon Sign Sagittarius

am . . . .

pm . . . .
It might be best for the moment to suspend any major decision making – not because you are likely to make any mistakes but simply because you could be so busy dealing with matters that crop up more or less instantly. The Crab should be able to harness energy and use it to deal with physical tasks.

19 WEDNESDAY

Moon Age Day 7   Moon Sign Sagittarius

am . . . .

pm . . . .
There is now a great need for you to see what lies around the next bend or over every wall. You are not only curious but can also be quite ingenious and can turn your fertile mind in just about any direction. Even if you have made this an interesting week, things could grind to a definite halt by tomorrow.

20 THURSDAY

Moon Age Day 8   Moon Sign Capricorn

am . . . .

pm . . . .
This has potential to be a much quieter day, and if the lunar low is preventing you from making the sort of progress you were starting to take for granted, you may have to work that much harder to gain your objectives. When matters can be left alone for a couple of days you might be well advised to put them aside.

21 FRIDAY

Moon Age Day 9   Moon Sign Capricorn

am . . . .

pm . . . .
Beware of pushing too hard because you may not get what you want and might only exhaust yourself trying to do so. Rather you should be clearing the decks for actions that come later, whilst also getting some rest and relaxation. Learning to read the stars and the way they guide you is easier for the Crab than for most.

22 SATURDAY

Moon Age Day 10   Moon Sign Capricorn

am . . . .

pm . . . .
For the first part of today at least you will still be inclined to hold back. By just after the middle of the day the Moon moves on, leaving you with an afternoon and evening that should be far more optimistic and eventful. Social possibilities look especially good, encouraging you to think about an interesting night out.

23 SUNDAY

Moon Age Day 11   Moon Sign Aquarius

am . . . .

pm . . . .
Personal and professional aims become much more achievable under present trends, and if you happen to work at the weekend you can make great use of what the planets are offering. Even if you are not committed to work you are in a position to find constructive things to do that contribute to your life.

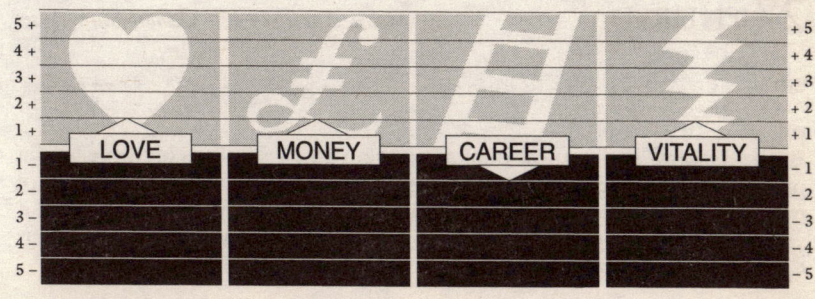

24 MONDAY
Moon Age Day 12   Moon Sign Aquarius

am . . . .

pm . . . .
This would be an excellent time during which to take a break of some
sort. It might be rather late for a holiday but if you have one planned for
this time, you couldn't have chosen better. It isn't that you lack vitality
or a sense of purpose, merely that you may now feel the call of the next
horizon and a need to ring the changes somehow.

25 TUESDAY
Moon Age Day 13   Moon Sign Pisces

am . . . .

pm . . . .
What happens now depends almost entirely on the way you approach
situations. All too often you leave the decision making to others and
simply tag along for the ride. If you can stay out in front and make the
running yourself, adventure and excitement are there for the taking. You
can afford to be very direct in conversation.

26 WEDNESDAY
Moon Age Day 14   Moon Sign Pisces

am . . . .

pm . . . .
You would be wise to exercise just a little caution when it comes to
money so you can avoid spending unwisely on something that would be
better left until later. Before you make any purchase you should ask
yourself if this is something you really need and then whether the article
in question represents good value.

27 THURSDAY
Moon Age Day 15   Moon Sign Aries

am . . . .

pm . . . .
Both personal and professional aims seem to be easily achievable under
present trends, and you can use this to put you in a cheerful frame of
mind. Although gambling is never to be recommended it is true that
your level of general good luck is higher than usual at the moment.
Confidence to say and do the right thing is not lacking.

28 FRIDAY
Moon Age Day 16   Moon Sign Aries

am . . . .

pm . . . .
Trends assist you to put a large amount of effort today into improving both your finances and your personal life. Perhaps the two are related in some way but it is clear that you are able to look ahead and try to improve things generally. Don't try too hard when it comes to persuading others that you know best.

29 SATURDAY
Moon Age Day 17   Moon Sign Taurus

am . . . .

pm . . . .
It seems that you have tremendous mental energy today and you should relish any sort of challenge that stretches your mind. At the same time you could be more physically invigorated than has been the case for quite a while and show yourself willing to push the bounds of what you once thought was possible for you.

30 SUNDAY
Moon Age Day 18   Moon Sign Taurus

am . . . .

pm . . . .
The present position of Venus in your solar chart encourages you to turn your attention towards love and you shouldn't find it at all hard to sweep someone off their feet. You can attract many compliments around now and can make the most of present trends by simply accepting that people are genuine in what they say.

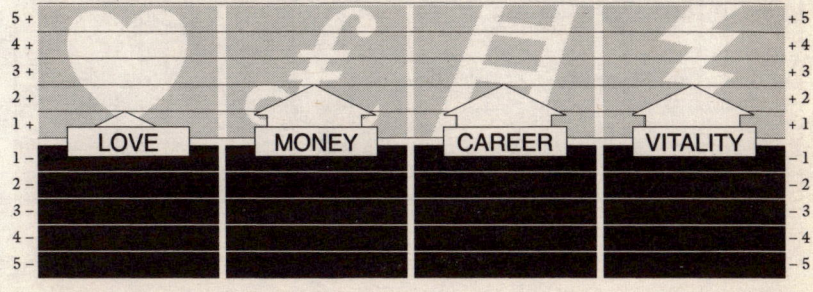

October 2007

YOUR MONTH AT A GLANCE

⊕ = Opportunities are around ⊖ = Be on the defensive ● = Life is pretty ordinary

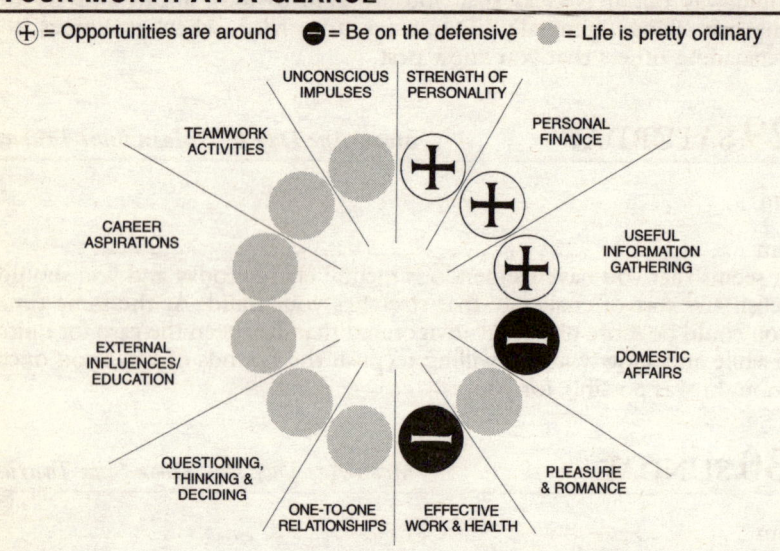

- STRENGTH OF PERSONALITY
- PERSONAL FINANCE
- USEFUL INFORMATION GATHERING
- DOMESTIC AFFAIRS
- PLEASURE & ROMANCE
- EFFECTIVE WORK & HEALTH
- ONE-TO-ONE RELATIONSHIPS
- QUESTIONING, THINKING & DECIDING
- EXTERNAL INFLUENCES/EDUCATION
- CAREER ASPIRATIONS
- TEAMWORK ACTIVITIES
- UNCONSCIOUS IMPULSES

OCTOBER HIGHS AND LOWS

Here I show you how the rhythms of the Moon will affect you this month. Like the tide, your energies and abilities will rise and fall with its pattern. When it is above the centre line, go for it, when it is below, you should be resting.

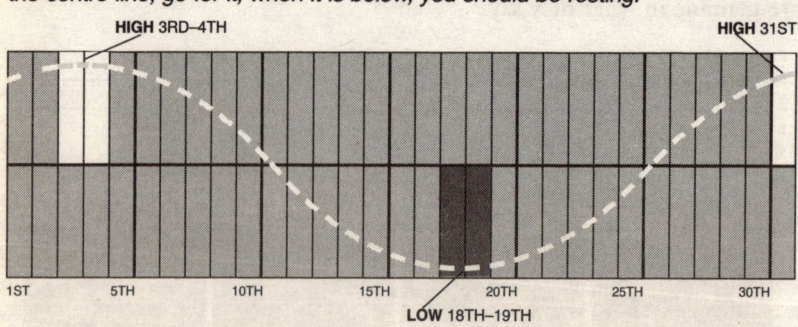

HIGH 3RD–4TH

HIGH 31ST

LOW 18TH–19TH

1ST 5TH 10TH 15TH 20TH 25TH 30TH

1 MONDAY
Moon Age Day 19   Moon Sign Gemini

am ....

pm ....
You seem to be able to take life pretty much in your stride at the beginning of this new week and new month. October will offer you significant incentives and you could do worse that to make a start by deciding what it is you want most from life. Concentrated effort definitely works best in the day ahead.

2 TUESDAY
Moon Age Day 20   Moon Sign Gemini

am ....

pm ....
It pays to be up-front in all your dealings with the world at large. Don't have secrets and be as open as you can with everyone. The more others are instinctively aware that you are as pure as the driven snow, the greater should be the trust they have in you. Be careful that you don't buy a pig in a poke if you are out shopping.

3 WEDNESDAY
Moon Age Day 21   Moon Sign Cancer

am ....

pm ....
The Moon returns to your zodiac sign and since it is also your ruling planet, that's got to be good news. Take all your vitality today and aim it towards a dream that has been in your mind for quite some time. Even the impossible is not beyond the bounds of credibility and at the very least you could achieve a great compromise.

4 THURSDAY
Moon Age Day 22   Moon Sign Cancer

am ....

pm ....
You continue to be able to show a very positive face to the world at large. If you are seeking freedom, this is the time to make your pitch. In a physical sense you have scope to be energetic and to take hurdles that would usually hold you back. Most important of all is the truly magnetic and attractive personality you can display.

5 FRIDAY
Moon Age Day 23   Moon Sign Leo

am . . . .

pm . . . .
Someone, somewhere could be making you feel good with the attention they are heaping upon you. This might cause you to be slightly suspicious and although it is sensible to be on your guard, you might be going over the top. Why not accept that many people think you are great?

6 SATURDAY
Moon Age Day 24   Moon Sign Leo

am . . . .

pm . . . .
If specific demands are being made of you at the moment, you might decide to spend some time sorting these out before you please yourself. It would be easy to get irritable with those you see as failing before they even try and you might even decide that in some cases it would be easier simply to do things yourself.

7 SUNDAY
Moon Age Day 25   Moon Sign Leo

am . . . .

pm . . . .
Exciting times are possible ahead and it is worth taking a very close look at your finances in order to know whether you are in a position to spoil yourself in some way. Don't argue for your limitations or you will come face to face with them. It is better now to remain optimistic and to push forward in any way you can.

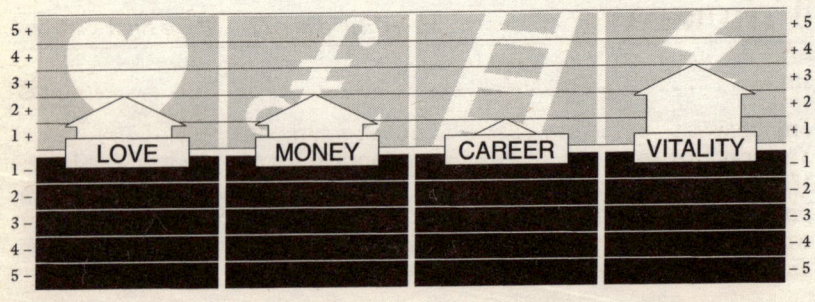

8 MONDAY
Moon Age Day 26   Moon Sign Virgo

am . . . .

pm . . . .
Communication issues are highlighted at the moment and you could learn something that is to your definite advantage. This is a time to be in the know in a number of different ways, both for your own sake and with regard to your chief concern, which is always your family.

9 TUESDAY
Moon Age Day 27   Moon Sign Virgo

am . . . .

pm . . . .
Things look good on the career front and especially so for those of you who have recently started a new job or else swapped responsibilities in some way. In addition to work you have a personal life too, and you shouldn't forget about it under present trends. Finding the right compliments to really knock someone off their feet could work wonders.

10 WEDNESDAY
Moon Age Day 28   Moon Sign Libra

am . . . .

pm . . . .
Hearth and home are important at the moment, but you may find your mind and your life somewhat split if a part of you also wants to be out and about. It ought to be possible to reach some sort of compromise with yourself and to share your time. Beware of getting tied down with petty rules and regulations today.

11 THURSDAY
Moon Age Day 0   Moon Sign Libra

am . . . .

pm . . . .
Trends assist you to turn your mind outward, away from the insular concerns that sometimes captivate you and towards the excitement that lies beyond your own front door. Despite the late date this would be an excellent time to take a break, and an impromptu holiday arranged around now could be good.

12 FRIDAY ☿ *Moon Age Day 1 Moon Sign Libra*

am . . . .

pm . . . .
The level of success you have at work today is specifically tied to who you know and the way you use the contacts you already have. Not that you need to focus your mind exclusively in the direction of your career. New social interests are there for the taking, probably ones to which friends introduce you.

13 SATURDAY ☿ *Moon Age Day 2 Moon Sign Scorpio*

am . . . .

pm . . . .
At this time social matters and group-based activities could well be attracting your attention. You might be quite keen to try something new and can easily enlist the support of your partner or maybe a good friend if you don't want to go it alone. There may be moments today when you will need to explain yourself.

14 SUNDAY ☿ *Moon Age Day 3 Moon Sign Scorpio*

am . . . .

pm . . . .
Time spent with friends today is certainly not wasted. If you display the warm and caring side of your nature, people should love to have you around. Attitude is very important if you are facing a change to your plans and have to adapt quickly. Self-belief isn't always present for the Crab, but you can make sure it is now.

LOVE	MONEY	CAREER	VITALITY

15 MONDAY ☿ *Moon Age Day 4 Moon Sign Sagittarius*

am ....

pm ....
There is a strong pioneering quality about you today, mainly encouraged by the position and aspects of the Moon in your solar chart. Rather than allowing yourself to be bulldozed into taking directions that are not of your own choosing, why not show that even easy-going Cancer can be stubborn on occasions?

16 TUESDAY ☿ *Moon Age Day 5 Moon Sign Sagittarius*

am ....

pm ....
There are signs that any journey you undertake today could be fortunate and even exciting. It doesn't really matter whether you are moving about in connection with work or simply for social reasons – the change should do you good. Look out for personalities who enter your life around this time and make the most of their presence.

17 WEDNESDAY ☿ *Moon Age Day 6 Moon Sign Sagittarius*

am ....

pm ....
The way to success in terms of personal relationships means keeping your feet on the ground and adopting a realistic attitude towards events. This may not prove to be the best romantic interlude of the month, but if it isn't, you can reassure yourself that this is through no fault of yours. The behaviour of others has a part to play.

18 THURSDAY ☿ *Moon Age Day 7 Moon Sign Capricorn*

am ....

pm ....
You can afford to take life at a slower pace today and to allow others to make some of the running. If you have been in a position to offer another person some sort of training, it would now be sensible to see how well they can do. The lunar low might deter you from pushing ahead in a personal sense.

19 FRIDAY ☿ *Moon Age Day 8 Moon Sign Capricorn*

am . . . .

pm . . . .
This is not a time during which you should be loading yourself down with too many burdens. The more you keep life light and airy, the less you should feel hampered by situations. The Crab is usually a big reader, and there won't be a better time this month to bury your head in a favourite book.

20 SATURDAY ☿ *Moon Age Day 9 Moon Sign Aquarius*

am . . . .

pm . . . .
The lunar low passes away and you can return to a more progressive frame of mind. Specific decisions made today, even if they don't appear too important at the time, could be extremely significant in the longer-term. For this reason you would be wise to concentrate and to avoid making mistakes.

21 SUNDAY ☿ *Moon Age Day 10 Moon Sign Aquarius*

am . . . .

pm . . . .
If you really want to have a pleasant day today it would be sensible to forget all about responsibilities and to enjoy yourself. This can be achieved best in the company of people you find relaxing to be with. Don't try to achieve anything important – simply settle down and appreciate the ride!

	LOVE	MONEY	CAREER	VITALITY
5 +				+ 5
4 +				+ 4
3 +				+ 3
2 +				+ 2
1 +				+ 1
1 -				- 1
2 -				- 2
3 -				- 3
4 -				- 4
5 -				- 5

22 MONDAY ☿ *Moon Age Day 11 Moon Sign Pisces*

am . . . .

pm . . . .
Your popularity could be at an all-time high, and that may prove to be especially useful to you. The people with whom you mix on a daily basis seem to have your best interests at heart and you can get them to move mountains to help you. It is at times such as this that you realise just how much you are appreciated.

23 TUESDAY ☿ *Moon Age Day 12 Moon Sign Pisces*

am . . . .

pm . . . .
A period of harmonious relationships is on offer and should continue throughout most of today. You can use it to make sure that friendships are secure and happy and that you are feeling generally content with your lot in life. The only slight fly in the ointment could be that you are in some ways too comfortable.

24 WEDNESDAY ☿ *Moon Age Day 13 Moon Sign Pisces*

am . . . .

pm . . . .
If you make instant decisions today you could live to regret the fact. A slower and steadier approach to most situations would now help, and even though you will occasionally be certain that you are right, you need to question your thinking. With just a little care, you can ensure things work out fine.

25 THURSDAY ☿ *Moon Age Day 14 Moon Sign Aries*

am . . . .

pm . . . .
The time has now come to adopt a higher profile. If you've had a few days during which you have been fairly quiet and willing to take on board what others think, now is a time for positive action. Don't be surprised today if you attract romantic attention of some sort.

26 FRIDAY ☿ *Moon Age Day 15* *Moon Sign Aries*

am . . . .

pm . . . .
You can afford to feel more independent and enthusiastic – a far cry from
the Crab who is sometimes on display. Although you still show great
sensitivity of nature, you should now be more willing to overturn
previous prejudices and to do what seems right to you. Not everyone will
agree, but that's life!

27 SATURDAY ☿ *Moon Age Day 16* *Moon Sign Taurus*

am . . . .

pm . . . .
There is scope for you to focus on the material side of life during this
weekend. If there is something you have been meaning to buy for your
home, this could be as good a time as any to search it out. From a social
point of view you might decide to stick to your inner circle around now.

28 SUNDAY ☿ *Moon Age Day 17* *Moon Sign Taurus*

am . . . .

pm . . . .
There are signs that relationships may not be working out quite the way
you had intended. If those you care about the most are determined to be
difficult, there might be very little you can do about the situation. It's
worth showing your usual understanding, because your patience is sure
to win out in the end.

	LOVE	MONEY	CAREER	VITALITY
5 +				+ 5
4 +				+ 4
3 +				+ 3
2 +				+ 2
1 +				+ 1
1 -				- 1
2 -				- 2
3 -				- 3
4 -				- 4
5 -				- 5

29 MONDAY   ☿   *Moon Age Day 18   Moon Sign Gemini*

am . . . .

pm . . . .
Instant decisions are possible but not too potentially fortunate whilst the
Moon occupies your solar twelfth house. In some way your mind could
be confused, because a part of you is determined to push forward, whilst
other components of your nature are telling you to wait in the shadows
until you are more certain of yourself.

30 TUESDAY   ☿   *Moon Age Day 19   Moon Sign Gemini*

am . . . .

pm . . . .
It's possible to remain steady in your thinking and actions, but this state
of affairs will not last beyond today. If you have time on your hands, it
might be sensible to clear the decks for the actions that come along
during Wednesday and Thursday. In personal attachments you need to
avoid being too pushy.

31 WEDNESDAY   ☿   *Moon Age Day 20   Moon Sign Cancer*

am . . . .

pm . . . .
You can afford to feel very independent and enthusiastic today – just the
right state of affairs to put your foot on the gas pedal of life and to make
good headway. If you are certain in your thinking and your actions, you
can make sure that no one gets in your way, and even usually awkward
types will follow your lead without question.

1 THURSDAY   ☿   *Moon Age Day 21   Moon Sign Cancer*

am . . . .

pm . . . .
The positive trends continue whilst the Moon occupies the zodiac sign of
Cancer, and this is a period during which you can make even unexpected
progress. Although you may sometimes be reticent to get rid of baggage
that has accumulated in your life, now is a time when you should be
much more willing to commit yourself to the future.

2 FRIDAY ☿ *Moon Age Day 22   Moon Sign Leo*

am . . . .

pm . . . .
It is towards possessions and the way you view them that your mind is
now encouraged to turn. You are entering a period during which 'things'
will be far less important. It is for this reason that clearing out your
cupboards and drawers can work wonders. For once the Crab could be
deciding that it's best to travel light.

3 SATURDAY *Moon Age Day 23   Moon Sign Leo*

am . . . .

pm . . . .
Getting others to follow your line of reasoning ought to be quite easy
today, not least because your powers of communication are to the fore.
Finding the right words should be child's play, even though you might
sometimes wonder at your own ingenuity. This is no time to maintain a
sense of proportion!

4 SUNDAY *Moon Age Day 24   Moon Sign Virgo*

am . . . .

pm . . . .
Getting ahead of the game shouldn't be difficult. It is on days such as this
that you have scope to realise your own intelligence and to use it to your
advantage. Of course you can help others on the way, but there are some
people around who seem determined to stick fast.

	LOVE	MONEY	CAREER	VITALITY
+5				
+4				
+3				
+2				
+1				

November

2007

YOUR MONTH AT A GLANCE

⊕ = Opportunities are around ⊖ = Be on the defensive ● = Life is pretty ordinary

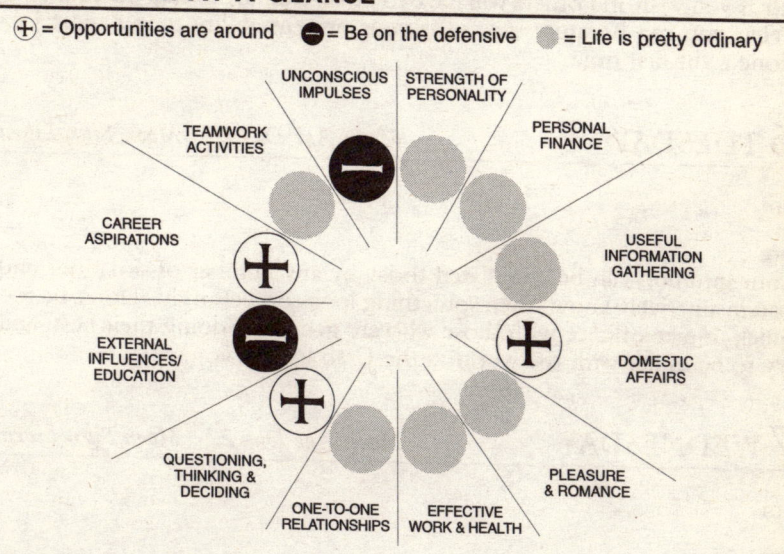

- UNCONSCIOUS IMPULSES ⊖
- STRENGTH OF PERSONALITY ●
- TEAMWORK ACTIVITIES ●
- PERSONAL FINANCE ●
- CAREER ASPIRATIONS ⊕
- USEFUL INFORMATION GATHERING ●
- EXTERNAL INFLUENCES/ EDUCATION ⊖
- DOMESTIC AFFAIRS ⊕
- QUESTIONING, THINKING & DECIDING ⊕
- PLEASURE & ROMANCE
- ONE-TO-ONE RELATIONSHIPS ●
- EFFECTIVE WORK & HEALTH ●

NOVEMBER HIGHS AND LOWS

Here I show you how the rhythms of the Moon will affect you this month. Like the tide, your energies and abilities will rise and fall with its pattern. When it is above the centre line, go for it, when it is below, you should be resting.

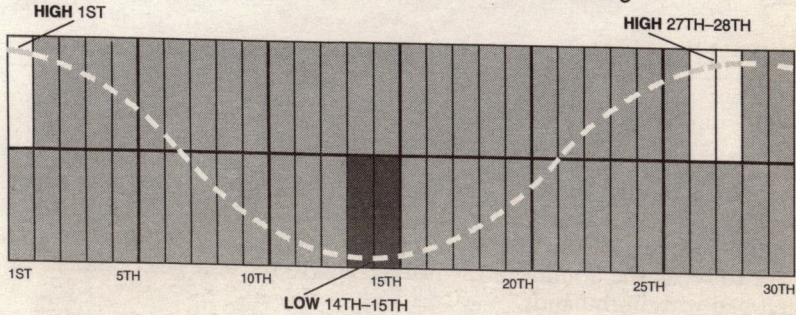

HIGH 1ST

HIGH 27TH–28TH

1ST 5TH 10TH 15TH 20TH 25TH 30TH

LOW 14TH–15TH

5 MONDAY
Moon Age Day 25   Moon Sign Virgo

am . . . .

pm . . . .
Where tasks have to be dealt with today, the signs are that you want to do things your own way. You might even be a little cranky if things don't go as you wish and others will have to be careful not to step on your toes. What you can be quite sure of is your present ability to get most jobs done right first time.

6 TUESDAY
Moon Age Day 26   Moon Sign Libra

am . . . .

pm . . . .
Your intuition can be stimulated today by any number of situations and you instinctively know when something looks or feels right. Don't be too quick to take offence with those who are genuinely doing their best, and try to be as fair with the world as the Crab usually is.

7 WEDNESDAY
Moon Age Day 27   Moon Sign Libra

am . . . .

pm . . . .
The present position of Mercury in your solar chart assists in all matters to do with communication. Where you have had difficulty getting your message across you can now find ways and means to explain yourself. This has potential to be a better day in terms of personal attachments and romance in particular.

8 THURSDAY
Moon Age Day 28   Moon Sign Libra

am . . . .

pm . . . .
It looks as though the Crab can be something of an explorer now and it is clear that you want to know what makes matters tick. This might not be the best part of the year to take a journey, but any opportunity you have to break the bounds of the normal and to see new places should be grabbed with both hands.

9 FRIDAY

Moon Age Day 0   Moon Sign Scorpio

am . . . .

pm . . . .
It is your social life that has the most to offer right now, and trends help you to get in just the right frame of mind to start something new, possibly with a group or in some way associated with your locality. Routines are best dealt with early in the day, leaving you more time later in which to please yourself.

10 SATURDAY

Moon Age Day 1   Moon Sign Scorpio

am . . . .

pm . . . .
If you have to approach others today in order to gain the assistance you need to do things that seem important, don't forget to be grateful and to show the fact. The Crab can be just slightly offhand right now, and that could lead to a little resentment. You should have the confidence to broach a difficult subject.

11 SUNDAY

Moon Age Day 2   Moon Sign Sagittarius

am . . . .

pm . . . .
Twosomes are well highlighted under present trends and this would be the best part of the week to cement relationships that are important to you. For once Cancer may not want to go it alone, and even if you are still quite happy with your own company, in the main you are probably happier to have others on board.

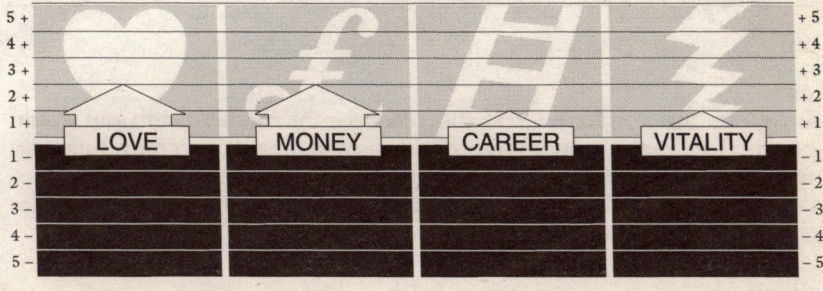

12 MONDAY
Moon Age Day 3   Moon Sign Sagittarius

am . . . .

pm . . . .
Friendships can be great fun at the beginning of this new working week and you have every opportunity to turn colleagues into pals. Trends show new people entering your life a good deal around now, and you have scope to make sure that at least one person becomes someone who will be important to you for years to come.

13 TUESDAY
Moon Age Day 4   Moon Sign Sagittarius

am . . . .

pm . . . .
You can afford to enjoy helping others today and to go to great lengths to please those around you – even people you don't know too well. This might be a good time during which to ask for a few favours, and Tuesday should also be ideal for gradually breaking down anything that has been a difficult situation.

14 WEDNESDAY
Moon Age Day 5   Moon Sign Capricorn

am . . . .

pm . . . .
With the lunar low coming along you shouldn't be afraid to slow the pace of life significantly. Your powers of discrimination may be more limited and it might also be easy to run out of energy. This is not an ideal day to embark on any new project that takes both stamina and self-belief.

15 THURSDAY
Moon Age Day 6   Moon Sign Capricorn

am . . . .

pm . . . .
It appears that you have a very short fuse for the moment, and you would be wise to count to ten in your dealings with people who tend to annoy you at the best of times. If you can't rely on the world at large, why not fall back on your own resources? The Crab could now be much quieter than of late.

16 FRIDAY
Moon Age Day 7   Moon Sign Aquarius

am ....

pm ....
You are now entering a more emotional period and a time during which you have a chance to talk about the deepest of issues. The inner workings of the Cancerian mind is a closed book, sometimes even to you, but trends now assist you to share these unexplored regions with someone else.

17 SATURDAY
Moon Age Day 8   Moon Sign Aquarius

am ....

pm ....
Chances are that you will now be making use of the help you can gain from others and may be able to achieve a closeness with a particular individual that has eluded you in the past. This could be because they are quite vulnerable at present, whilst you can be more honest and direct than might sometimes be the case.

18 SUNDAY
Moon Age Day 9   Moon Sign Aquarius

am ....

pm ....
Even if you are content with your own company for the next couple of days, this doesn't mean you have to be either miserable or particularly withdrawn. It's just that if there are things that need to be done, you should instinctively realise that matters can be sorted quicker if you go it alone.

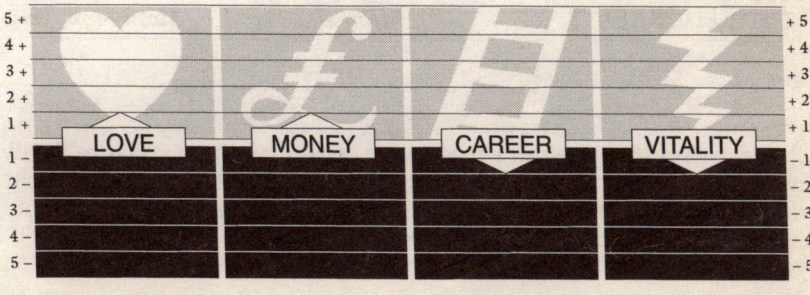

19 MONDAY

Moon Age Day 10   Moon Sign Pisces

am . . . .

pm . . . .
This is probably the best day of the month to choose to be with loved ones, and even if the everyday responsibilities of your life are still present, it is those intimate moments that count for the most. Don't worry if you still show a tendency to be reflective and quiet. You can make the most important people in your life understand.

20 TUESDAY

Moon Age Day 11   Moon Sign Pisces

am . . . .

pm . . . .
Money might not be the most important factor in your life at present, but it does have its part to play, and it's worth being aware of this fact now. Both medium- and long-term plans for increasing your wealth are favoured, and you should be quite happy to look at new and potentially lucrative possibilities.

21 WEDNESDAY

Moon Age Day 12   Moon Sign Aries

am . . . .

pm . . . .
You may well prefer time spent away from emotional demands today and can afford to show a light and airy approach to life generally. There may not be time for too much reflection in any case and the thought of having to untangle the personal mess someone else is in probably won't be too appealing.

22 THURSDAY

Moon Age Day 13   Moon Sign Aries

am . . . .

pm . . . .
Bear in mind that you can't trust every person you meet today and will need to be on your guard if you are not to be duped in some way. Rely on your instincts and don't overrule these with what seems like common sense. There is a little voice inside you that offers the very best advice and you would be wise to listen to it now.

23 FRIDAY
Moon Age Day 14   Moon Sign Taurus

am . . . .

pm . . . .
What a good day this would be for discussions and debates. Your wit is potentially razor-sharp and you will be able to make just about anyone laugh, which is halfway to gaining your objective. You could even be somewhat calculating in your approach at the moment, but if everyone wins in the end, does it matter?

24 SATURDAY
Moon Age Day 15   Moon Sign Taurus

am . . . .

pm . . . .
From being self-protective and thinking much more than usual about your own interests, you are now suddenly prompted to drop back into the more normal way of thinking for the Crab. This means being happy to exploit much of your energy in loving and protecting the people who are most important to you, both family and friends.

25 SUNDAY
Moon Age Day 16   Moon Sign Gemini

am . . . .

pm . . . .
This is a great time to be with the ones you care about the most, whether you are doing something practical or simply having fun. You should be able to find something to do that stimulates your intellect, whilst at the same time proving to quite educational. Trends assist you to forge new long-term interests now.

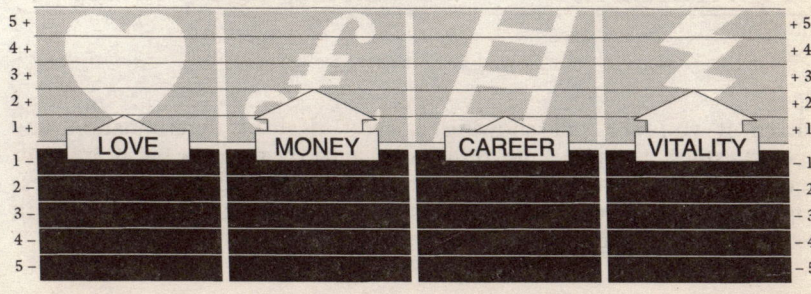

26 MONDAY
Moon Age Day 17   Moon Sign Gemini

am . . . .

pm . . . .
This may be a good time to withdraw somewhat, not because you are
miserable or out of sorts with yourself in any way, but simply because you
now work best on your own. These periods of self-imposed isolation are
not at all unusual for you, and this one is inspired by the position of the
Sun in your solar twelfth house.

27 TUESDAY
Moon Age Day 18   Moon Sign Cancer

am . . . .

pm . . . .
You can now afford to put new plans into operation and to break down
barriers that have existed in a specific area of your life for some time. You
can be like an irrepressible battering ram and you needn't
stop until you have achieved your objectives. This is the power of the
lunar high.

28 WEDNESDAY
Moon Age Day 19   Moon Sign Cancer

am . . . .

pm . . . .
Once again you can make great gains by putting new plans of action into
operation right now. Don't wait to be asked because you could lose the
power of the moment. Now is the time to ask for what you want and
maybe to take it in any case if those around you refuse to listen.

29 THURSDAY
Moon Age Day 20   Moon Sign Leo

am . . . .

pm . . . .
Even if you are still showing a great deal of determination and
perseverance it may not be quite as easy today to forge the important
connections you really want to make. Maybe others are less
approachable, or it could simply be that you are picking on the wrong
sort of people in the first place.

30 FRIDAY

Moon Age Day 21   Moon Sign Leo

am . . . .

pm . . . .
A day to concentrate on a specific issue, and not get too carried away with the insignificant details of life that don't really count for anything. Friendships prove to be very important and new casual attachments are possible for some Crabs. Getting really close to someone could be a different matter, and might prove difficult.

1 SATURDAY

Moon Age Day 22   Moon Sign Virgo

am . . . .

pm . . . .
You can now attract great generosity of spirit from others at the start of December, perhaps in return for favours you have done them in the past. Even if you are not actively looking for support, it is there all the same. Your mind is very questioning at present and especially with regard to issues that have a bearing on your home or locality.

2 SUNDAY

Moon Age Day 23   Moon Sign Virgo

am . . . .

pm . . . .
With a slight change of emphasis in terms of planetary influences it is now possible for you to confuse others with what you are both saying and doing. It's worth taking just a little time out to explain yourself because this can make all the difference. If you were looking for a peaceful Sunday, you could be somewhat disappointed!

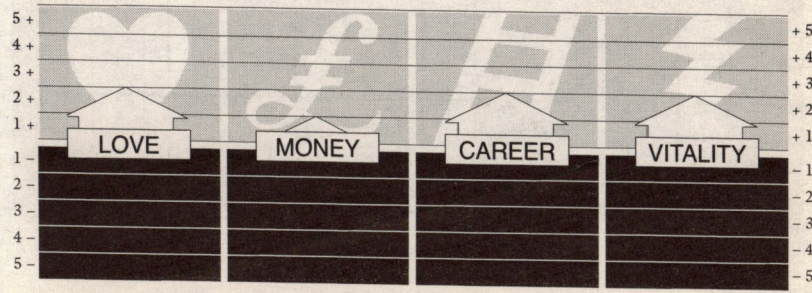

December

2007

YOUR MONTH AT A GLANCE

⊕ = Opportunities are around   ⊖ = Be on the defensive   ⬤ = Life is pretty ordinary

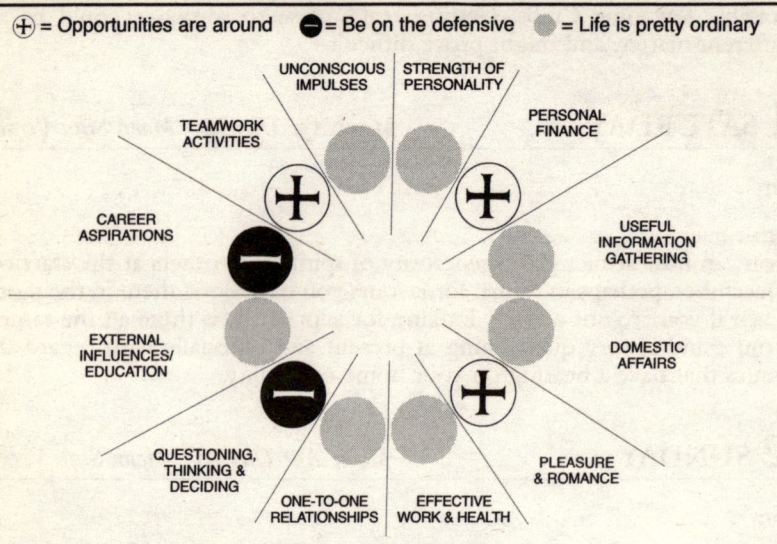

TEAMWORK ACTIVITIES
UNCONSCIOUS IMPULSES
STRENGTH OF PERSONALITY
PERSONAL FINANCE
CAREER ASPIRATIONS
USEFUL INFORMATION GATHERING
EXTERNAL INFLUENCES/ EDUCATION
DOMESTIC AFFAIRS
QUESTIONING, THINKING & DECIDING
ONE-TO-ONE RELATIONSHIPS
EFFECTIVE WORK & HEALTH
PLEASURE & ROMANCE

DECEMBER HIGHS AND LOWS

Here I show you how the rhythms of the Moon will affect you this month. Like the tide, your energies and abilities will rise and fall with its pattern. When it is above the centre line, go for it, when it is below, you should be resting.

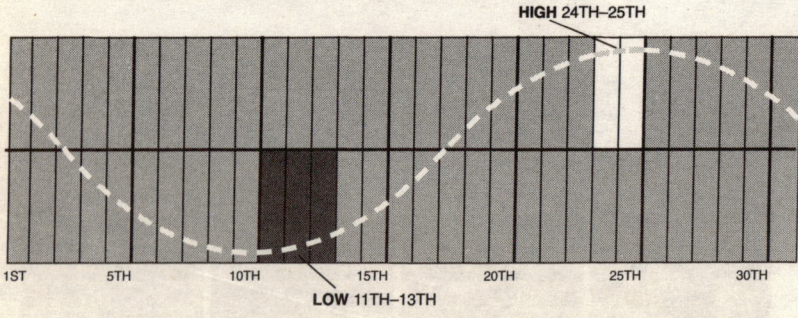

HIGH 24TH–25TH

1ST   5TH   10TH   15TH   20TH   25TH   30TH

LOW 11TH–13TH

3 MONDAY
Moon Age Day 24   Moon Sign Virgo

am . . . .

pm . . . .
There are signs that others want to be generous to you at the moment,
and you would do well to accept any offers that are made. What people
are doing is trying to repay you for the many kindnesses you have shown
to them, and you can take this as proof of the sort of person you are.

4 TUESDAY
Moon Age Day 25   Moon Sign Libra

am . . . .

pm . . . .
Optimism should remain generally high under present trends and you
might decide this would be a good time to push your luck just a little.
There are some real advantages to be had at work and at the same time
you can make the most of some slightly better financial luck than has
been the case recently.

5 WEDNESDAY
Moon Age Day 26   Moon Sign Libra

am . . . .

pm . . . .
There is a tendency now towards greater intimacy, even with people who
have been slightly distant in the past. Nevertheless you can remain
generally adventurous and might even decide to try something that has
seemed intimidating in the past. By this evening you could well be
organising social events for later in the month.

6 THURSDAY
Moon Age Day 27   Moon Sign Scorpio

am . . . .

pm . . . .
A day to look out for some good fortune in financial matters and to
spread your money around a little if you sense this is the right way to
proceed. As usual you need to rely heavily on your intuition, especially
when it comes to assessing whether people who are only now entering
your life are really trustworthy.

7 FRIDAY
Moon Age Day 28   Moon Sign Scorpio

am . . . .

pm . . . .
You should have a good instinctive understanding of people's motivation today and will not be easily fooled by anyone who has the clear intention of pulling the wool over your eyes. What could really annoy you is jargon and red tape, because your penetrating mind wants to go straight to the heart of any matter.

8 SATURDAY
Moon Age Day 29   Moon Sign Scorpio

am . . . .

pm . . . .
Trends suggest that personal matters may need a greater amount of thought than you have offered them so far this week, and the weekend doubtless offers you the opportunity to look at a number of issues in greater detail. This is not a day to rush your fences and you can afford to be more pensive than of late.

9 SUNDAY
Moon Age Day 0   Moon Sign Sagittarius

am . . . .

pm . . . .
If you really want to get on today you will have to put in a good deal more effort than might sometimes be the case. On the other hand, you should probably ask yourself if this might not be an ideal day to relax a little and to enjoy the entertainment that is brought to life by the antics of family members and friends.

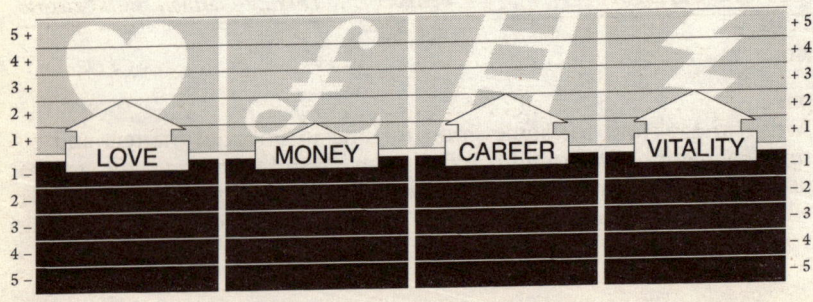

10 MONDAY

Moon Age Day 1   Moon Sign Sagittarius

am . . . .

pm . . . .
A favourable time to turn your attention to the material world. With everything to play for at the start of a new working week you will want to be up early and getting on with a number of different jobs. This is just as well because some notable delays are possible by tomorrow.

11 TUESDAY

Moon Age Day 2   Moon Sign Capricorn

am . . . .

pm . . . .
The lunar low could well be a time of detachment and a two-day period during which you are not really connected to the world at large in the way you have been so far this month. Your best response is to treat this as a period for rest and relaxation and be willing to allow your friends to take some of the necessary strain.

12 WEDNESDAY

Moon Age Day 3   Moon Sign Capricorn

am . . . .

pm . . . .
Group situations can prove to be especially rewarding, even if you decide to take something of a back seat for the moment. Although you sometimes use the period of the lunar low in order to retreat into yourself, this may not be the case today. On the contrary, trends encourage you to seek out some company.

13 THURSDAY

Moon Age Day 4   Moon Sign Capricorn

am . . . .

pm . . . .
Even if today starts quietly, by the time lunchtime arrives you should be right back in the groove and anxious to make headway again. Romance seems to be very important under present trends and it's worth spending at least part of today telling someone just how important they are to you.

14 FRIDAY
Moon Age Day 5   Moon Sign Aquarius

am . . . .

pm . . . .
This may well turn out to be a day of hectic comings and goings. Keeping up with the general flow of life might not be at all easy, especially if the people around you seem to be doing everything they can to confuse matters. Rather than causing you irritation or distress, this situation can be seen as quite funny.

15 SATURDAY
Moon Age Day 6   Moon Sign Aquarius

am . . . .

pm . . . .
Although your vitality could sag somewhat at times throughout today, in the main you should be keen to get on with life and anxious to show your most positive face to most situations. Keep abreast of local news and views and don't forget a particular job that has been hanging over you for most of the week.

16 SUNDAY
Moon Age Day 7   Moon Sign Pisces

am . . . .

pm . . . .
This may be the first real time during December that you have been able to give some time to thinking specifically about Christmas. Don't forget those all-important invitations, and make sure that family gatherings are adequately organised. If there is one sign that needs to have the festive season sorted, it's yours.

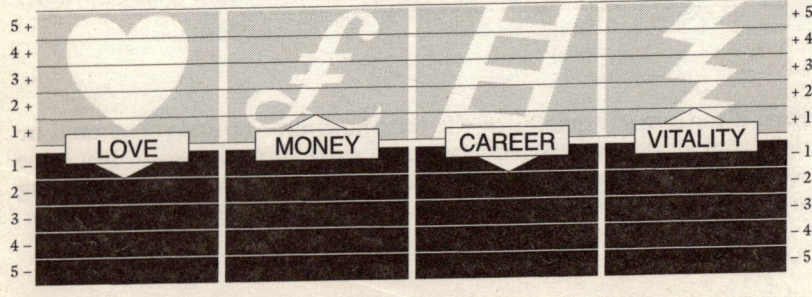

17 MONDAY
Moon Age Day 8   Moon Sign Pisces

am . . . .

pm . . . .
Your love life is definitely favoured under present planetary trends, and those Crabs who are between relationships can use the run-up to Christmas to provide the embryo of something new and special. At work you might find a few frustrations developing, but you have the ability to take these in your stride.

18 TUESDAY
Moon Age Day 9   Moon Sign Aries

am . . . .

pm . . . .
You now have the knack of making sure your desires turn out pretty much the way you wish, even if you sometimes have to take a rather tortuous path in order to get things done. There is much humour about at the moment, and you may well be in a more happy-go-lucky frame of mind than has been possible so far this month.

19 WEDNESDAY
Moon Age Day 10   Moon Sign Aries

am . . . .

pm . . . .
You ought to be able to take advantage of more fortunate financial trends that crop up around now, and might also be pleased to lend a hand in the slightly difficult situations that surround certain friends. Routines can be boring, which is why you might decide to ring the changes whenever possible.

20 THURSDAY
Moon Age Day 11   Moon Sign Taurus

am . . . .

pm . . . .
If there is a little more money around than you expected, why not hang onto it? With Christmas in view there is a danger you will be blowing everything you have on presents, but this could prove to be a mistake. Not least you may well have a chance to discover some amazing bargains if you wait for just a day or two.

21 FRIDAY   *Moon Age Day 12*   *Moon Sign Taurus*

am ....

pm ....
You can display your versatility at the moment and you can tackle routine and usual jobs in very new ways. Although you have one eye on the upcoming festivities, you should also be very committed to the everyday requirements life has of you. There are some real advantages on offer in your personal life.

22 SATURDAY   *Moon Age Day 13*   *Moon Sign Gemini*

am ....

pm ....
Simply being yourself is the best key to happiness at the present time, though with the Moon in your solar twelfth house you could be slightly quieter than of late and anxious to spend an hour or two entirely alone. Splitting your time between solitary interludes and the needs of your family is the balancing act for today.

23 SUNDAY   *Moon Age Day 14*   *Moon Sign Gemini*

am ....

pm ....
Even if you seem to be slightly below par when it comes to communicating, in the main you can get on better today than you might have expected. Why not see if you can get others to help you out with jobs that are irritating or boring? You can afford to respond positively to the little favours others afford you.

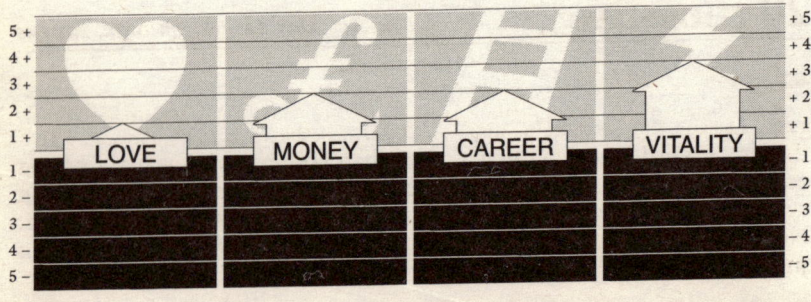

24 MONDAY   *Moon Age Day 15   Moon Sign Cancer*

am . . . .

pm . . . .
Christmas Eve brings the lunar high and helps you to make this one of
the most positive and happy Christmas periods you have experienced for
some time. Get the difficult jobs out of the way early in the day and if
possible save some time to get to the shops. Most people hate town on a
Christmas Eve, but not you. Look out for some bargains.

25 TUESDAY   *Moon Age Day 16   Moon Sign Cancer*

am . . . .

pm . . . .
You have so much going for you at the moment that it might be difficult
to know in which way to turn your attention. Not only do you have
plenty of charm and humour to make everyone else happy on this
Christmas Day, you should be able to achieve a level of contentment that
even the Crab rarely experiences.

26 WEDNESDAY   *Moon Age Day 17   Moon Sign Leo*

am . . . .

pm . . . .
You can make sure this is an exuberant period, when you don't have to
work very hard in order to get what you want from life. There are some
interesting personalities about and you could be making a new friend.
Romance is well highlighted and today could be the best day of
Christmas in some respects.

27 THURSDAY   *Moon Age Day 18   Moon Sign Leo*

am . . . .

pm . . . .
A chance word in the right direction could see you well set in terms of
plans for the New Year. Even if you are fully enjoying what the festive
season has to offer, it's also worth keeping one eye firmly placed on the
future. In every respect you can now keep more balls in the air than a
juggler.

28 FRIDAY

Moon Age Day 19   Moon Sign Leo

am . . . .

pm . . . .
There are signs that involvement with friends could prove to be more complicated and difficult today than has been the case at any stage during December. In all probability this has little or nothing to do with you personally, but may be down to the complications in the lives of others. Be prepared to offer your special advice.

29 SATURDAY

Moon Age Day 20   Moon Sign Virgo

am . . . .

pm . . . .
This would be a really good time to discuss things with family members. Maybe you are thinking about holidays for next year, or else a major change at home that will come along in the spring. Don't confuse issues any more than is necessary, and perhaps find the time to look carefully at all those Christmas presents!

30 SUNDAY

Moon Age Day 21   Moon Sign Virgo

am . . . .

pm . . . .
There are definitely helpful elements about on the path to progress today, even if some of them are disguised rather well. You have what it takes to play the detective at present and to find out how everything works. Stand by for some real surprises when it comes to the lives and thoughts of your friends.

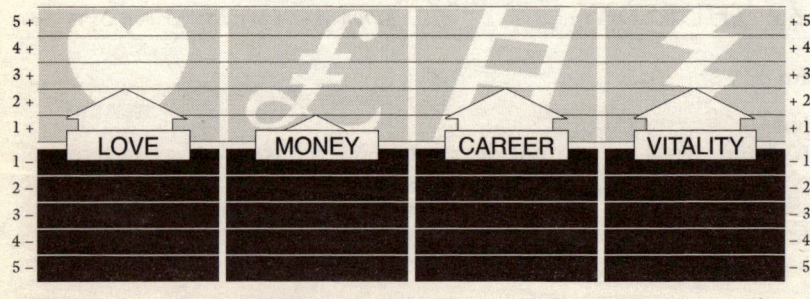

31 MONDAY

Moon Age Day 22   Moon Sign Libra

am . . . .

pm . . . .

There are a few actions around today that could prove to be rather self-defeating. Maybe you should content yourself by going with the flow, because no matter how hard you try it is unlikely that you will make much practical headway. New Year's resolutions may well start before the day is over.

RISING SIGNS FOR CANCER

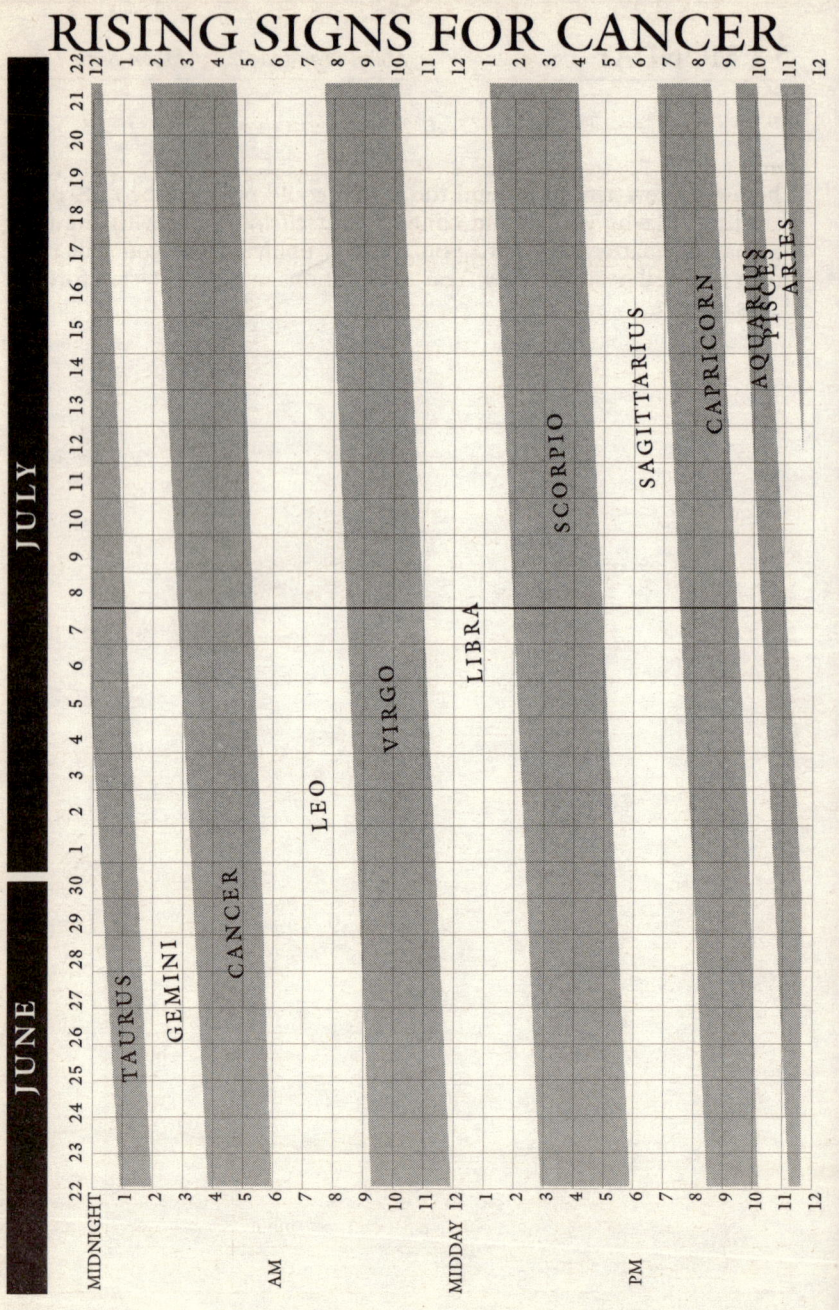

THE ZODIAC, PLANETS AND CORRESPONDENCES

The Earth revolves around the Sun once every calendar year, so when viewed from Earth the Sun appears in a different part of the sky as the year progresses. In astrology, these parts of the sky are divided into the signs of the zodiac and this means that the signs are organised in a circle. The circle begins with Aries and ends with Pisces.

Taking the zodiac sign as a starting point, astrologers then work with all the positions of planets, stars and many other factors to calculate horoscopes and birth charts and tell us what the stars have in store for us.

The table below shows the planets and Elements for each of the signs of the zodiac. Each sign belongs to one of the four Elements: Fire, Air, Earth or Water. Fire signs are creative and enthusiastic; Air signs are mentally active and thoughtful; Earth signs are constructive and practical; Water signs are emotional and have strong feelings.

It also shows the metals and gemstones associated with, or corresponding with, each sign. The correspondence is made when a metal or stone possesses properties that are held in common with a particular sign of the zodiac.

Finally, the table shows the opposite of each star sign – this is the opposite sign in the astrological circle.

Placed	Sign	Symbol	Element	Planet	Metal	Stone	Opposite
1	Aries	Ram	Fire	Mars	Iron	Bloodstone	Libra
2	Taurus	Bull	Earth	Venus	Copper	Sapphire	Scorpio
3	Gemini	Twins	Air	Mercury	Mercury	Tiger's Eye	Sagittarius
4	Cancer	Crab	Water	Moon	Silver	Pearl	Capricorn
5	Leo	Lion	Fire	Sun	Gold	Ruby	Aquarius
6	Virgo	Maiden	Earth	Mercury	Mercury	Sardonyx	Pisces
7	Libra	Scales	Air	Venus	Copper	Sapphire	Aries
8	Scorpio	Scorpion	Water	Pluto	Plutonium	Jasper	Taurus
9	Sagittarius	Archer	Fire	Jupiter	Tin	Topaz	Gemini
10	Capricorn	Goat	Earth	Saturn	Lead	Black Onyx	Cancer
11	Aquarius	Waterbearer	Air	Uranus	Uranium	Amethyst	Leo
12	Pisces	Fishes	Water	Neptune	Tin	Moonstone	Virgo

Foulsham books can be found in all
good bookshops or direct from
www.foulsham.com